Date Due

Oscar Wilde

THE IMPORTANCE OF BEING EARNEST

**Introduction and questions by
Tim Bezant**

Heinemann Educational Publishers
Halley Court, Jordan Hill, Oxford OX2 8EJ
Part of Harcourt Education

First published 1899
First published in the *Hereford Plays* series by Heinemann Educational 1970
First published in the *Heinemann Plays* series 1994

    03 04 13 12 11 10 9 8

A catalogue record for this book is available from the British Library on request.
ISBN 0 435 23303 3

Cover design by Keith Pointing

Designed by Jeffrey White Creative Associates

Typeset by Taurus Graphics, Kidlington, Oxon

Printed in the UK by Clays Ltd, St Ives plc

CONTENTS

PREFACE

In this edition of *The Importance of Being Earnest*, you will find notes, questions and activities to help in studying the play in class, particularly at GCSE level.

The introduction provides background information on the author, the historical context of the play and the circumstances and impact of its first production. It examines in detail the two main characters and outlines the play's plot and performance.

The activities at the end of the book range from straight-forward *Keeping Track* questions which can be tackled at the end of each act to focus close attention on what is happening in the play, through more detailed work on characters and themes in *Explorations*, to more advanced discussion questions under *Criticism*.

There is also a bibliography with details of Oscar Wilde's work and some recent works of criticism and biography.

If you are already using the Hereford edition of *The Importance of Being Earnest*, you will find that the page numbering in the actual playscript is the same, allowing the two editions to be easily used side by side.

INTRODUCTION

Oscar Wilde

Oscar Fingal O'Flahertie Wills Wilde was born on 16 October 1854 in Dublin, Ireland. His father was a successful and famous physician, his mother a poet. After being tutored at home, he attended Portora School and Trinity College Dublin from where, at the age of nineteen, he won a scholarship to read Classics at Magdalen College, Oxford.

At Oxford Wilde was a brilliant scholar, winning the Newdigate Prize for English verse and, eventually, taking a first class degree. It was during his time at Oxford that he came under the influence of Walter Pater, a don at the University, whose ideas he took up and defined as what became known as 'aestheticism'. This was the pursuit and enjoyment of beauty for its own sake, whether in art or in life itself. Wilde practised what was preached, attracting attention to himself by his flamboyant dress and by his brilliant wit in conversation.

On graduation from Oxford in 1878 Wilde settled in London, where his reputation had preceded him. He quickly became established in society circles, being an attraction at dinner parties because of his wit and his style. Although determined to write for the stage, he earned his living writing as a critic and commentator. This led in turn in 1882 to a lecture tour of America where his first play *Vera*, was performed unsuccessfully in New York the following year. On his return to London he met and married Constance Lloyd, by whom he had two sons. He was now well known as a lecturer, reviewer, critic and editor and at the same time he was establishing himself as a successful writer and teller of short stories and fairy tales.

By now, however, Wilde was living a double life. In 1886 he had met and been seduced by Robert Ross. Unknown to his wife, Wilde now became involved in a series of homosexual relationships at a time when homosexuality was still a criminal offence punishable by imprisonment. Wilde's fascination with the forbidden was highlighted by his only novel, *The Picture of Dorian Gray*, published in 1890, which was controversially received. Throughout this time he continued to nurture his ambitions as a playwright and when George Alexander, a London producer, took over St James's Theatre in 1890, he invited Wilde to write for him.

Lady Windermere's Fan, produced in 1892, was a resounding success. Wilde followed it in 1893 with *A Woman of No Importance* which, although less liked by the critics, was just as successful at the box office. Wilde was now well established as a popular playwright; he compounded his successes with the opening of *An Ideal Husband* and *The Importance of Being Earnest* in January and February 1895 respectively.

What should have been Wilde's triumph now became his tragedy. Since 1892 Wilde had been engaged in an affair with Lord Alfred Douglas, son of the Marquess of Queensbury, who disapproved not only of his son's sexuality but especially of Wilde as his partner. Having already challenged Wilde over the affair in his own home, he had attempted, unsuccessfully, to disrupt the opening of *The Importance of Being Earnest*. Frustrated, he now left Wilde a calling-card at Wilde's club inscribed with an insulting message. Wilde deemed the message to be libellous and took Queensbury to court. In the case which followed, however, Wilde's homosexuality was publicly revealed. He lost his libel case and in the trials for indecency which followed was found guilty and sentenced to two years' imprisonment with hard labour. While his plays continued to run, his name was erased from their posters.

Wilde served his sentence at Reading Gaol. His time in prison broke both his health and his spirit. On his release in 1897 he left England to live under an assumed name in Paris. *The Ballad of Reading Gaol*, written in the year of his release, reflected upon the nature of his prison experiences but was his last serious work. Visited only occasionally by friends from England, Wilde slipped into decline, poverty and ill-health. He died on 30 November, 1900, his friend Robert Ross at his bedside.

The Theatrical Context

The London theatre for which Wilde wrote was experiencing a rebirth in the 1890s as it found itself to be newly socially respectable and fashionable. The late Victorian era was a period of material prosperity, fostered by the traditional Victorian values of hard work, diligence and thrift. As the prosperous upper and middle classes sought to reap the rewards of their efforts, so the theatre became more popular both as a means of entertainment and of social progress and improvement for those who could afford to attend.

Simultaneously, the major theatrical producers were concerned to make theatre going attractive by making it more of a social event. To this end theatres were renovated and plushly and comfortably refurbished. Foyers were provided in which the theatre patrons' sense of occasion could be heightened. Producers and theatre owners such as the actor-managers Henry Irving, Charles Wyndham and George Alexander maintained control over all aspects of their theatre's environments, from what was seen on the stage to what appeared on the posters, vying with each other in competition. Alexander's St James's Theatre, where *The Importance of Being Earnest* was first staged, was acknowledged as 'the established home of polite comedy'.

New audiences and theatres demanded new writers: as well as Wilde, writers such as Arthur Pinero, Henry Arthur Jones and George Bernard Shaw were popular. The Savoy operas of Gilbert and Sullivan (in which Wilde was once parodied) were also immensely successful. The main trends in the drama of his time were for comedies of manners and for social problem plays, but in all drama, the plays fundamentally presented characters and situations which the upper and middle class audiences could recognise and identify and of which they could approve. After all, if attending the theatre was to maintain its respectability as a recognised and approved social pastime, and if the theatre itself was to continue to profit by this, it had to subscribe to the moral and social values held by those it sought to attract and entertain.

The Importance of Being Earnest

The Importance of Being Earnest was written in August and September 1894 during a family holiday in Worthing, near Brighton, while Wilde was enjoying the fame and success brought by *Lady Windermere's Fan* and *A Woman of No Importance*. In its original form the play was in four, rather than three acts, but George Alexander felt that this version was too long. Wilde complied with his request and the present Act Two is a combination of Acts Two and Three of the original version.

Wilde's philosophy in what was to be his last play was 'that we should treat all trivial things very seriously, and all the serious things of life with sincere and studied triviality'. This represented an almost paradoxical inversion of normal, conventional everyday values and, as a result, created considerable scope for humour. Wilde himself described the play as a 'somewhat farcical comedy' and indeed the play does contain many farcical elements: dual and mistaken identities, disguise, inscriptions which incriminate the characters involved, guilty secrets from the past which are suddenly revealed in the present, and a revelatory conclusion in which the characters achieve their happy endings.

However, by inverting and overturning the conventional values of late Victorian society, Wilde was freed to parody and criticise them. While the title of the play proclaims the importance of being earnest, serious and solemn, the content of the play itself subverts such an attitude. The characters' wilful playfulness is expressed in Wilde's characteristically witty dialogue, the principal features of which are epigram (a short, pointed, pithy expression of an opinion) and paradox (an apparently self-contradictory, nonsense statement, founded upon truth). Through the action of the play, arising from the characters' attitudes, traditionally serious and earnest features of late Victorian society such as the receiving of guests, the taking of afternoon tea, the proposal of marriage, the interview of an intended fiancé, as well as the attitudes to money, manners and class upon which upper-class and aristocratic life was founded, are all progressively mocked. The ultimate irony lay in the fact that the audience found itself laughing at precisely those values to which it subscribed.

The majority of critics greeted the play rapturously. H. G. Wells pronounced it to be 'very good nonsense, excellent fooling'; Hamilton Fyfe found it 'extraordinarily funny'. Other critics found the play harder to deal with: Bernard Shaw found that there was no true humanity in the play, and that all that was memorable was its wit. William Archer wrote: 'What can a poor critic do with a play which ... is nothing but an absolutely wilful expression of an irrepressibly witty personality?'

Only A B Walkley in *The Speaker* attempted to analyse the nature and humour of the play, which he found generated 'the most delightful form of laughter'.

> You are in a world that is real yet fantastic ... the common sense has been left out ... Wilde makes his personages ridiculous but ... he does not ridicule them ... . And the result is that you have something like real life in detail yet, in sum, absolutely unlike it;

> the familiar materials of life are shaken up ... and rearranged in a
> strange, unnatural pattern. It is this combination of the natural
> and the absurd which causes our laughter.

It is this capacity of the play as a comedy, entirely self-contained, to generate laughter, that has maintained the presence of *The Importance of Being Earnest* upon both the British and World Stage. It has been revived frequently, both in London and elsewhere, including a production at London's National Theatre in 1982; and it has been filmed successfully, for both the cinema and for television.

In Performance

The Importance of Being Earnest is clearly a play of its period: a successful production must aim to present 'something like real life in detail' or, at the very least, conjure in the audience's imagination the upper-class and aristocratic background against which the action is set.

Three settings are required: while neither is described in detail each would need to be precisely realised. Algernon's bachelor flat in Half Moon Street, then as now a fashionable and exclusive part of London, is required to be 'luxuriously and artistically furnished': at the very least, it would need to look as if Algernon spared no expense in designing his room to reflect his personality. Act Two is set in the garden at Jack's 'place in the country': clearly the size and substantial nature of 'The Manor House, Woolton, Hertfordshire' would need to be suggested to the audience. Finally, Act Three is set in the morning-room of the Manor House: again, a suitably impressive setting, reflecting the social background, would be required. All three settings would require a high degree of realism in order to establish the context for the action of the play.

Both the characters and the plot of *The Importance of Being Earnest* have been criticised for an absurdity and a lack of seriousness which is unrealistic: this is, of course, the quality from which the action and the success of the play springs. The actors portraying the characters to an audience must convey no awareness of the absurdities of either the characters or the action: both they and the audience must willingly suspend their disbelief. Simultaneously, however, the characters must not be presented as caricatures: within the conventions and action of the play itself, they must be presented as realistically as possible.

Essentially, the characters are straightforward and uncomplicated, both for actors to present and for audiences to understand. Both Jack and Algernon are bachelor men about town, who lead lives of ease and financial security which allow them to please themselves. Jack has the responsibility of being Cecily's guardian, which is a restraining influence, is intent upon marriage to Gwendolen, and has the worry of the uncertainty of his parentage, but Algernon is a truly free agent, able to come and go as he pleases both in town and in the country, using his sick 'friend' Bunbury as an excuse as he feels necessary, the only constraint on his behaviour being his Aunt Augusta's opinion of him. This is usually disapproving, for Lady Bracknell is Wilde's version of the middle-aged, upper-class lady of distinction, full of her own self-importance, who speaks with an air of incontrovertible authority and who is, no doubt, the head of the family.

Her daughter Gwendolen is the object of Jack's affections, just as Jack's ward Cecily becomes the object of Algernon's. Gwendolen has the advantage of living in London and being a part of society, while Cecily is still being tutored towards taking her place there. Both, however, are strong-willed young ladies, being well-born and well-bred and possessing a determination which leads to their initial dislike of each other, and to their alliance in Act Three, when the source of their confusion becomes clear.

Miss Prism and Canon Chasuble are more functional characters. Miss Prism, as Cecily's precise governess, ought to take more care in directing her education but is too easily distracted from it herself: she is also vital as the play moves to its denouement when she once again falls under Lady Bracknell's withering spell. Canon Chasuble, the object of Miss Prism's distraction, provides further light relief from the main plot as he courts Miss Prism and arranges Jack's and Algy's baptisms. Both are stock characters from farce, more conventional objects for amusement. The servants, Lane and Merriman, serve their functions with a degree of wit which, in Lane's case, helps to set the tone of the play.

All of the characters are brought together by a single, unifying factor: that they all speak 'pure and undiluted Wildese'. None of the characters speaks in an individual manner that characterises them in particular: rather, they all speak in the same highly cultivated, highly sophisticated style that characterises the play as a whole. This high degree of cultivation would also, in a successful production, extend to the quality of movement of the characters. As has already been noted, the late Victorian era adhered to strict codes of manners and behaviour in the highest social circles and this would need to be reflected in a modern performance, especially now that such codes are no longer applicable.

Finally, the nature of the comedy too is cultivated: as will become clear in a reading of the play, the audience is required to listen intelligently if the humour is to succeed. Sir John Gielgud, writing of his production of the play, noted that 'The pace of the comedy must be leisurely, mannered ... but the wit must appear spontaneous, though self-conscious'. The high pace of farce would be wholly inappropriate: ultimately, *The Importance of Being Earnest,* is a comedy of sophistication and style and the pace of performance would need to be pitched to show the characters at their best: sophisticated, stylish and wholly self-aware of their own importance. The only allowances required thereafter would be for the audience's laughter.

Reading the Play

All plays are written to be performed or, at the very least, read aloud. This is certainly true of *The Importance of Being Earnest.* Only in reading the play aloud will the nature and quality of the wit and its expression in highly cultivated, formulated and constructed dialogue become clear. This will in turn highlight the interplay and interaction of the characters and allow for a fuller understanding of their attitudes and motivations to be developed.

The play is formally constructed of three acts but, within each act, various 'scenes' are readily identifiable: these are usually marked by the entrance or exit of a particular character. This lends particular parts of the play to detailed study and to reading and rehearsing in small groups. A useful approach is to read sections aloud first of all to understand the content and the action; then explore and experiment with the text to discover more depth and understanding of the characters, the humour and the action and how they combine in order to make the play effective and successful.

Following the play text you will find two series of questions entitled *Keeping Track* and *Explorations. Keeping Track* is intended to help your understanding of the characters and the action as the play develops and can be used while reading the play for the first time. *Explorations* are more detailed and demanding questions organised according to the characters, themes, performance and criticism. The questions in this section may lead to coursework assignments or examination practice. All the questions are designed to stimulate knowledge, understanding and, hopefully, enjoyment of the play.

Tim Bezant

List of Characters

JOHN WORTHING

ALGERNON MONCRIEFF

REV. CANON CHASUBLE

MERRIMAN

LANE

LADY BRACKNELL

GWENDOLEN FAIRFAX

CECILY CARDEW

MISS PRISM

THE IMPORTANCE OF BEING EARNEST

ACT ONE

The morning-room in ALGERNON'S *flat in Half Moon Street. The room is luxuriously and artistically furnished. The sound of a piano is heard in the adjoining room.*

LANE *is arranging afternoon tea on the table and, after the music has ceased,* ALGERNON *enters.*

ALGERNON   Did you hear what I was playing, Lane?

    LANE   I didn't think it polite to listen, sir.

ALGERNON   I'm sorry for that, for your sake. I don't play accurately – anyone can play accurately – but I play with wonderful expression. As far as the piano is concerned, sentiment is my forte. I keep science for Life.

    LANE   Yes, sir.

ALGERNON   And, speaking of the science of Life, have you got the cucumber sandwiches cut for Lady Bracknell?

    LANE   Yes, sir. (*Hands them on a salver.*)

ALGERNON   (*inspects them, takes two, and sits down on the sofa*) Oh! ... by the way. Lane, I see from your book that on Thursday night, when Lord Shoreman and Mr Worthing were dining with me, eight bottles of champagne are entered as having been consumed.

    LANE   Yes, sir; eight bottles and a pint.

ALGERNON   Why is it that at a bachelor's establishment the servants invariably drink the champagne? I ask merely for information.

    LANE   I attribute it to the superior quality of the wine, sir. I have often observed that in married households the champagne is rarely of a first-rate brand.

ALGERNON Good heavens! Is marriage so demoralizing as that?

LANE I believe it *is* a very pleasant state, sir. I have had very little experience of it myself up to the present. I have only been married once. That was in consequence of a misunderstanding between myself and a young person.

ALGERNON (*languidly*) I don't know that I am much interested in your family life, Lane.

LANE No, sir; it is not a very interesting subject. I never think of it myself.

ALGERNON Very natural, I am sure. That will do, Lane, thank you.

LANE Thank you, sir (LANE *goes out.*)

ALGERNON Lane's views on marriage seem somewhat lax. Really, if the lower orders don't set us a good example, what on earth is the use of them? They seem, as a class, to have absolutely no sense of moral responsibility. (*Enter* LANE.)

LANE Mr Ernest Worthing. (*Enter* JACK, LANE *goes out.*)

ALGERNON How are you, my dear Ernest? What brings you up to town?

JACK Oh, pleasure, pleasure! What else should bring one anywhere? Eating as usual, I see, Algy!

ALGERNON (*stiffly*) I believe it is customary in good society to take some slight refreshment at five o'clock. Where have you been since last Thursday?

JACK (*sitting down on the sofa*) In the country.

ALGERNON What on earth do you do there?

JACK (*pulling off his gloves*) When one is in town one amuses oneself. When one is in the country one amuses other people. It is excessively boring.

ALGERNON And who are the people you amuse?

JACK (*airily*) Oh, neighbours, neighbours.

ALGERNON Got nice neighbours in your part of Shropshire?

JACK Perfectly horrid! Never speak to one of them.

ALGERNON How immensely you must amuse them! (*Goes over and takes sandwich.*) By the way, Shropshire is your county, is it not?

JACK Eh? Shropshire? Yes, of course. Hallo! Why all these cups? Why cucumber sandwiches? Why such reckless extravagance in one so young? Who is coming to tea?

ALGERNON Oh! merely Aunt Augusta and Gwendolen.

JACK How perfectly delightful!

ALGERNON Yes, that is all very well; but I am afraid Aunt Augusta won't quite approve of your being here.

JACK May I ask why?

ALGERNON My dear fellow, the way you flirt with Gwendolen is perfectly disgraceful. It is almost as bad as the way Gwendolen flirts with you.

JACK I am in love with Gwendolen. I have come up to town expressly to propose to her.

ALGERNON I thought you had come up for pleasure? ... I call that business.

JACK How utterly unromantic you are!

ALGERNON I really don't see anything romantic in proposing. It is very romantic to be in love. But there is nothing romantic about a definite proposal. Why, one may be accepted. One usually is, I believe. Then the excitement is all over. The very essence of romance is uncertainty. If ever I get married, I'll certainly try to forget the fact.

JACK I have no doubt about that, dear Algy. The Divorce Court was specially invented for people whose memories are so curiously constituted.

ALGERNON Oh! there is no use speculating on that subject. Divorces are made in heaven – (JACK *puts out his hand to take a sandwich.* ALGERNON *at once interferes.*) Please don't touch the cucumber sandwiches. They are ordered specially for Aunt Augusta. (*Takes one and eats it.*)

JACK Well, you have been eating them all the time.

ALGERNON That is quite a different matter. She is my aunt.

(*Takes plate from below.*) Have some bread and butter. The bread and butter is for Gwendolen. Gwendolen is devoted to bread and butter.

JACK (*advancing to table and helping himself*) And very good bread and butter it is too.

ALGERNON Well, my dear fellow, you need not eat as if you were going to eat it all. You behave as if you were married to her already. You are not married to her already, and I don't think you ever will be.

JACK Why on earth do you say that?

ALGERNON Well, in the first place girls never marry the men they flirt with. Girls don't think it right.

JACK Oh, that is nonsense!

ALGERNON It isn't. It is a great truth. It accounts for the extraordinary number of bachelors that one sees all over the place. In the second place, I don't give my consent.

JACK Your consent!

ALGERNON My dear fellow, Gwendolen is my first cousin. And before I allow you to marry her, you will have to clear up the whole question of Cecily. (*Rings bell.*)

JACK Cecily! What on earth do you mean? What do you mean, Algy, by Cecily? I don't know anyone of the name of Cecily. (*Enter* LANE.)

ALGERNON Bring me that cigarette case Mr Worthing left in the smoking-room the last time he dined here.

LANE Yes, sir. (LANE *goes out.*)

JACK Do you mean to say you have had my cigarette case all this time? I wish to goodness you had let me know. I have been writing frantic letters to Scotland Yard about it. I was very nearly offering a large reward.

ALGERNON Well, I wish you would offer one. I happen to be more than usually hard up.

JACK There is no good offering a large reward now that the thing is found. (*Enter* LANE *with the cigarette case on a salver.* ALGERNON *takes it at once.* LANE *goes out.*)

ALGERNON   I think that is rather mean of you, Ernest. I must say.
(*Opens case and examines it.*) However, it makes no
matter, for, now that I look at the inscription inside, I
find that the thing isn't yours after all.

JACK   Of course it's mine (*Moving to him.*) You have seen
me with it a hundred times, and you have no right
whatsoever to read what is written inside. It is a very
ungentlemanly thing to read a private cigarette case.

ALGERNON   Oh! it is absurd to have a hard-and-fast rule about
what one should read and what one shouldn't. More
than half of modern culture depends on what one
shouldn't read.

JACK   I am quite aware of the fact, and I don't propose to
discuss modern culture. It isn't the sort of thing one
should talk of in private. I simply want my cigarette
case back.

ALGERNON   Yes, but this isn't your cigarette case. This cigarette
case is a present from someone of the name of Cecily,
and you said you didn't know anyone of that name.

JACK   Well, if you want to know, Cecily happens to be my
aunt.

ALGERNON   Your aunt!

JACK   Yes. Charming old lady she is, too. Lives at Tunbridge
Wells. Just give it back to me, Algy.

ALGERNON   (*retreating to back of sofa*) But why does she call
herself Cecily if she is your aunt and lives at
Tunbridge Wells? (*Reading.*) 'From little Cecily with
her fondest love.'

JACK   (*moving to sofa and kneeling upon it*) My dear fellow,
what on earth is there in that? Some aunts are tall,
some aunts are not tall. That is a matter that surely an
aunt may be allowed to decide for herself. You seem
to think that every aunt should be exactly like your
aunt! That is absurd! For heaven's sake give me back
my cigarette case. (*Follows* ALGERNON *round the room.*)

ALGERNON   Yes. But why does your aunt call you her
uncle? 'From little Cecily, with her fondest love to her

dear Uncle Jack.' There is no objection, I admit, to an aunt being a small aunt, but why an aunt, no matter what her size may be, should call her own nephew her uncle, I can't quite make out. Besides, your name isn't Jack at all; it is Ernest.

JACK It isn't Ernest, it's Jack.

ALGERNON You have always told me it was Ernest. I have introduced you to everyone as Ernest. You answer to the name of Ernest. You look as if your name was Ernest. You are the most earnest looking person I ever saw in my life. It is perfectly absurd your saying that your name isn't Ernest. It's on your cards. Here is one of them. (*Taking it from case.*) 'Mr Ernest Worthing, B. 4, The Albany.' I'll keep this as a proof that your name is Ernest if ever you attempt to deny it to me, or to Gwendolen, or to anyone else. (*Puts the card in his pocket.*)

JACK Well, my name is Ernest in town and Jack in the country, and the cigarette case was given to me in the country.

ALGERNON Yes, but that does not account for the fact that your small Aunt Cecily, who lives at Tunbridge Wells, calls you her dear uncle. Come, old boy, you had much better have the thing out at once.

JACK My dear Algy, you talk exactly as if you were a dentist. It is very vulgar to talk like a dentist when one isn't a dentist. It produces a false impression.

ALGERNON Well, that is exactly what dentists always do. Now, go on! Tell me the whole thing. I may mention that I have always suspected you of being a confirmed and secret Bunburyist; and I am quite sure of it now.

JACK Bunburyist? What on earth do you mean by a Bunburyist?

ALGERNON I'll reveal to you the meaning of that incomparable expression as soon as you are kind enough to inform me why you are Ernest in town and Jack in the country.

JACK Well, produce my cigarette case first.

ALGERNON Here it is. (*Hands cigarette case.*) Now produce your explanation and pray make it improbable. (*Sits on sofa.*)

JACK My dear fellow, there is nothing improbable about my explanation at all. In fact it's perfectly ordinary. Old Mr Thomas Cardew, who adopted me when I was a little boy, made me in his will guardian to his granddaughter, Miss Cecily Cardew. Cecily, who addresses me as her uncle from motives of respect that you could not possibly appreciate, lives at my place in the country under the charge of her admirable governess, Miss Prism.

ALGERNON Where is that place in the country, by the way?

JACK That is nothing to you, dear boy. You are not going to be invited . . . I may tell you candidly that the place is not in Shropshire.

ALGERNON I suspected that, my dear fellow! I have Bunburyed all over Shropshire on two separate occasions. Now, go on. Why are you Ernest in town and Jack in the country?

JACK My dear Algy, I don't know whether you will be able to understand my real motives. You are hardly serious enough. When one is placed in the position of guardian, one has to adopt a very high moral tone on all subjects. It's one's duty to do so. And as a high moral tone can hardly be said to conduce very much to either one's health or one's happiness, in order to get up to town I have always pretended to have a younger brother of the name of Ernest, who lives in the Albany, and gets into the most dreadful scrapes. That, my dear Algy, is the whole truth pure and simple.

ALGERNON The truth is rarely pure and never simple. Modern life would be very tedious if it were either, and modern literature a complete impossibility!

JACK That wouldn't be at all a bad thing.

ALGERNON Literary criticism is not your forte, my dear fellow. Don't try it. You should leave that to people who haven't been at a University. They do it so well in the daily papers. What you really are is a Bunburyist. I was quite right in saying you were a Bunburyist. You are one of the most advanced Bunburyists I know.

JACK What on earth do you mean?

ALGERNON You have invented a very useful young brother called Ernest, in order that you may be able to come up to town as often as you like. I have invented an invaluable permanent invalid called Bunbury, in order that I may be able to go down into the country whenever I choose. Bunbury is perfectly invaluable. If it wasn't for Bunbury's extraordinary bad health, for instance, I wouldn't be able to dine with you at Willis's to-night, for I have been really engaged to Aunt Augusta for more than a week.

JACK I haven't asked you to dine with me anywhere to-night.

ALGERNON I know. You are absurdly careless about sending out invitations. It is very foolish of you. Nothing annoys people so much as not receiving invitations.

JACK You had much better dine with your Aunt Augusta.

ALGERNON I haven't the smallest intention of doing anything of the kind. To begin with, I dined there on Monday, and once a week is quite enough to dine with one's own relations. In the second place, whenever I do dine there I am always treated as a member of the family, and sent down with either no woman at all, or two. In the third place, I know perfectly well whom she will place me next to, tonight. She will place me next to Mary Farquhar, who always flirts with her own husband across the dinner-table. That is not very pleasant. Indeed, it is not even decent … and that sort of thing is enormously on the increase. The amount of women in London who flirt with their own husbands is perfectly scandalous. It looks so bad. It is simply washing one's clean linen in public. Besides, now that I know you to be a confirmed Bunburyist, I naturally want to talk to you about Bunburying. I want to tell you the rules.

JACK I'm not a Bunburyist at all. If Gwendolen accepts me, I am going to kill my brother, indeed I think I'll kill him in any case. Cecily is a little too much interested in him. It is rather a bore. So I am going to get rid of Ernest. And I strongly advise you to do the same with Mr ... with your invalid friend who has the absurd name.

ALGERNON Nothing will induce me to part with Bunbury, and if you ever get married, which seems to me extremely problematic, you will be very glad to know Bunbury. A man who marries without knowing Bunbury has a very tedious time of it.

JACK That is nonsense. If I marry a charming girl like Gwendolen, and she is the only girl I ever saw in my life that I would marry, I certainly won't want to know Bunbury.

ALGERNON Then your wife will. You don't seem to realize that in married life three is company and two is none.

JACK (*sententiously*) That, my dear young friend, is the theory that the corrupt French Drama has been propounding for the last fifty years.

ALGERNON Yes; and that the happy English home has proved in half the time.

JACK For heaven's sake, don't try to be cynical. It's perfectly easy to be cynical.

ALGERNON My dear fellow, it isn't easy to be anything nowadays. There's such a lot of beastly competition about. (*The sound of an electric bell is heard.*) Ah! that must be Aunt Augusta. Only relatives, or creditors, ever ring in that Wagnerian manner. Now, if I get her out of the way for ten minutes, so that you can have an opportunity for proposing to Gwendolen, may I dine with you to-night at Willis's?

JACK I suppose so, if you want to.

ALGERNON Yes, but you must be serious about it. I hate people who are not serious about meals. It is so shallow of them. (*Enter* LANE.)

LANE Lady Bracknell and Miss Fairfax. (ALGERNON *goes forward to meet them. Enter* LADY BRACKNELL *and* GWENDOLEN.)

LADY B. Good afternoon, dear Algernon, I hope you are behaving very well.

ALGERNON I'm feeling very well, Aunt Augusta.

LADY B. That's not quite the same thing. In fact the two things rarely go together. (*Sees* JACK *and bows to him with icy coldness.*)

ALGERNON (*to* GWENDOLEN) Dear me, you are smart!

GWENDOLEN I am always smart! Aren't I, Mr Worthing?

JACK You're quite perfect, Miss Fairfax.

GWENDOLEN Oh! I hope I am not that. It would leave no room for developments, and I intend to develop in many directions. (GWENDOLEN *and* JACK *sit down together in the corner.*)

LADY B. I'm sorry if we are a little late, Algernon, but I was obliged to call on dear Lady Harbury. I hadn't been there since her poor husband's death. I never saw a woman so altered; she looks quite twenty years younger. And now I'll have a cup of tea, and one of those nice cucumber sandwiches you promised me.

ALGERNON Certainly, Aunt Augusta. (*Goes over to tea-table.*)

LADY B. Won't you come and sit here, Gwendolen?

GWENDOLEN Thanks, mamma, I'm quite comfortable where I am.

ALGERNON (*picking up empty plate in horror*) Good heavens! Lane! Why are there no cucumber sandwiches? I ordered them specially.

LANE (*gravely*) There were no cucumbers in the market this morning, sir. I went down twice.

ALGERNON No cucumbers!

LANE No, sir. Not even for ready money.

ALGERNON That will do, Lane, thank you.

LANE Thank you, sir.

ALGERNON I am greatly distressed, Aunt Augusta, about there being no cucumbers, not even for ready money.

LADY B. It really makes no matter, Algernon. I had some crumpets with Lady Harbury, who seems to me to be living entirely for pleasure now.

ALGERNON I hear her hair has turned quite gold from grief.

LADY B. It certainly has changed its colour. From what cause I, of course, cannot say. (ALGERNON *crosses and hands tea.*) Thank you. I've quite a treat for you tonight, Algernon. I am going to send you down with Mary Farquhar. She is such a nice woman, and so attentive to her husband. It's delightful to watch them.

ALGERNON I am afraid, Aunt Augusta, I shall have to give up the pleasure of dining with you tonight after all.

LADY B. (*frowning*) I hope not, Algernon. It would put my table completely out. Your uncle would have to dine upstairs. Fortunately he is accustomed to that.

ALGERNON It is a great bore, and, I need hardly say, a terrible disappointment to me, but the fact is I have just had a telegram to say that my poor friend Bunbury is very ill again. (*Exchanges glances with* JACK.) They seem to think I should be with him.

LADY B. It is very strange. This Mr Bunbury seems to suffer from curiously bad health.

ALGERNON Yes; poor Bunbury is a dreadful invalid.

LADY B. Well, I must say, Algernon, that I think it is high time that Mr Bunbury made up his mind whether he was going to live or die. This shilly-shallying with the question is absurd. Nor do I in any way approve of the modern sympathy with invalids. I consider it morbid. Illness of any kind is hardly a thing to be encouraged in others. Health is the primary duty of life. I am always telling that to your poor uncle, but he never seems to take much notice ... as far as any improvement in his ailments goes. I should be obliged if you would ask Mr Bunbury, from me, to be kind enough not to have a relapse on Saturday, for I rely on you to arrange my music for me. It is my last reception, and one wants something that will encourage conversation, particularly at the end of the season when everyone has practically said whatever they had to say, which, in most cases, was probably not much.

ALGERNON I'll speak to Bunbury, Aunt Augusta, if he is still conscious, and I think I can promise you he'll be all right by Saturday. Of course the music is a great difficulty. You see, if one plays good music, people don't listen, and if one plays bad music, people don't talk. But I'll run over the programme I've drawn out, if you will kindly come into the next room for a moment.

LADY B. Thank you, Algernon. It is very thoughtful of you. (*Rising, and following* ALGERNON.) I'm sure the programme will be delightful, after a few expurgations. French songs I cannot possibly allow. People always seem to think that they are improper, and either looked shocked, which is vulgar, or laugh, which is worse. But German sounds a thoroughly respectable language, and indeed, I believe is so. Gwendolen, you will accompany me.

GWENDOLEN Certainly, mamma. (LADY BRACKNELL *and* ALGERNON *go into the music-room,* GWENDOLEN *remains behind.*)

JACK Charming day it has been, Miss Fairfax.

GWENDOLENPray don't talk to me about the weather, Mr Worthing. Whenever people talk to me about the weather, I always feel quite certain that they mean something else. And that makes me so nervous.

JACK   I do mean something else.

GWENDOLEN   I thought so. In fact, I am never wrong.

JACK   And I would like to be allowed to take advantage of Lady Bracknell's temporary absence... .

GWENDOLEN   I would certainly advise you to do so. Mamma has a way of coming back suddenly into a room that I have often had to speak to her about.

JACK   (*nervously*) Miss Fairfax, ever since I met you I have admired you more than any girl ... I have ever met since ... I met you.

GWENDOLEN   Yes, I am quite aware of the fact. And I often wish that in public, at any rate, you had been more demonstrative. For me you have always had an irresistable fascination. Even before I met you I was far from indifferent to you. (JACK *looks at her in amazement.*) We live, as I hope you know, Mr Worthing, in an age of ideals. The fact is constantly mentioned in the more expensive monthly magazines, and has reached the provincial pulpits I am told: and my ideal has always been to love someone of the name of Ernest. There is something in that name that inspires absolute confidence. The moment Algernon first mentioned to me that he had a friend called Ernest, I knew I was destined to love you.

JACK   You really love me, Gwendolen?

GWENDOLEN   Passionately!

JACK   Darling! You don't know how happy you've made me.

GWENDOLEN   My own Ernest!

JACK   But you don't really mean to say that you couldn't love me if my name wasn't Ernest?

GWENDOLEN   But your name is Ernest.

JACK   Yes, I know it is. But supposing it was something else? Do you mean to say you couldn't love me then?

GWENDOLEN   (*glibly*) Ah! that is clearly a metaphysical speculation, and like most metaphysical speculations has very little reference at all to the actual facts of real life, as we know them.

JACK Personally, darling, to speak quite candidly, I don't much care about the name of Ernest … I don't think the name suits me at all.

GWENDOLEN It suits you perfectly. It is a divine name. It has a music of its own. It produces vibrations.

JACK Well, really, Gwendolen, I must say that I think there are lots of other much nicer names. I think Jack, for instance, a charming name.

GWENDOLEN Jack? … No, there is very little music in the name Jack, if any at all, indeed. It does not thrill. It produces absolutely no vibrations… I have known several Jacks, and they all, without exception, were more than usually plain. Besides, Jack is a notorious domesticity for John! And I pity any woman who is married to a man called John. She would probably never be allowed to know the entrancing pleasure of a single moment's solitude. The only really safe name is Ernest.

JACK Gwendolen, I must get christened at once – I mean we must get married at once. There is no time to be lost.

GWENDOLEN Married, Mr Worthing?

JACK (*astounded*) Well … surely. You know that I love you, and you led me to believe, Miss Fairfax, that you were not absolutely indifferent to me.

GWENDOLEN I adore you. But you haven't proposed to me yet. Nothing has been said at all about marriage. The subject has not even been touched on.

JACK Well … may I propose to you now?

GWENDOLEN I think it would be an admirable opportunity. And to spare you any possible disappointment, Mr Worthing, I think it only fair to tell you quite frankly beforehand that I am fully determined to accept you.

JACK Gwendolen!

GWENDOLEN	Yes, Mr Worthing, what have you got to say to me?
JACK	You know what I have got to say to you.
GWENDOLEN	Yes, but you don't say it.
JACK	Gwendolen, will you marry me? (*Goes on his knees.*)
GWENDOLEN	Of course I will, darling. How long you have been about it! I am afraid you have had very little experience in how to propose.
JACK	My own one, I have never loved anyone in the world but you.
GWENDOLEN	Yes, but men often propose for practice. I know my brother Gerald does. All my girl-friends tell me so. What wonderfully blue eyes you have, Ernest! They are quite, quite blue. I hope you will always look at me just like that, especially when there are other people present.

(*Enter* LADY BRACKNELL.)

LADY B.	Mr Worthing! Rise, sir, from this semi-recumbent posture. It is most indecorous.
GWENDOLEN	Mamma! (*He tries to rise; she restrains him.*) I must beg you to retire. This is no place for you. Besides, Mr Worthing has not quite finished yet.
LADY B.	Finished what, may I ask?
GWENDOLEN	I am engaged to Mr Worthing, mamma. (*They rise together.*)
LADY B.	Pardon me, you are not engaged to anyone. When you do become engaged to someone, I, or your father, should his health permit him, will inform you of the fact. An engagement should come on a young girl as a surprise, pleasant or unpleasant, as the case may be. It is hardly a matter that she could be allowed to arrange for herself … And now I have a few questions to put to you, Mr Worthing. While I am making these inquiries, you, Gwendolen, will wait for me below in the carriage.
GWENDOLEN	(*reproachfully*) Mamma!

LADY B. In the carriage, Gwendolen! (GWENDOLEN *goes to the door. She and* JACK *blow kisses to each other behind* LADY BRACKNELL'S *back.* LADY BRACKNELL *looks vaguely about as if she could not understand what the noise was. Finally turns round.*) Gwendolen, the carriage!

GWENDOLEN Yes, mamma. (*Goes out, looking back at* JACK.)

LADY B. (*sitting down*) You can take a seat, Mr Worthing. (*Looks in her pocket for notebook and pencil.*)

JACK Thank you, Lady Bracknell, I prefer standing.

LADY B. (*pencil and notebook in hand*) I feel bound to tell you that you are not down on my list of eligible young men, although I have the same list as the dear Duchess of Bolton has. We work together, in fact. However, I am quite ready to enter your name, should your answers be what a really affectionate mother requires. Do you smoke?

JACK Well, yes, I must admit I smoke.

LADY B. I am glad to hear it. A man should always have an occupation of some kind. There are far too many idle men in London as it is. How old are you?

JACK Twenty-nine.

LADY B. A very good age to be married at. I have always been of the opinion that a man who desires to get married should know either everything or nothing. Which do you know?

JACK (*after some hesitation*) I know nothing, Lady Bracknell.

LADY B. I am pleased to hear it. I do not approve of anything that tampers with natural ignorance. Ignorance is like a delicate exotic fruit; touch it and the bloom is gone. The whole theory of modern education is radically unsound. Fortunately in England, at any rate, education produces no effect whatsoever. If it did, it would prove a serious danger to the upper classes, and probably lead to acts of violence in Grosvenor Square. What is your income?

JACK Between seven and eight thousand a year.

LADY B. (*makes a note in her book*) In land, or in investments?

JACK In investments, chiefly.

LADY B. That is satisfactory. What between the duties expected of one during one's lifetime, and the duties exacted from one after one's death, land has ceased to be either a profit or a pleasure. It gives one position, and prevents one from keeping it up. That's all that can be said about land.

JACK I have a country house with some land, of course, attached to it, about fifteen hundred acres, I believe; but I don't depend on that for my real income. In fact, as far as I can make out, the poachers are the only people who make anything out of it.

LADY B. A country house! How many bedrooms? Well, that point can be cleared up afterwards. You have a town house, I hope? A girl with a simple, unspoiled nature, like Gwendolen, could hardly be expected to reside in the country.

JACK Well, I own a house in Belgrave Square, but it is let by the year to Lady Bloxham. Of course, I can get it back whenever I like, at six months' notice.

LADY B. Lady Bloxham? I don't know her.

JACK Oh, she goes about very little. She is a lady considerably advanced in years.

LADY B. Ah, nowadays that is no guarantee of respectability of character. What number in Belgrave Square?

JACK 149.

LADY B. (*shaking her head*) The unfashionable side. I thought there was something. However, that could easily be altered.

JACK Do you mean the fashion, or the side?

LADY B. (*sternly*) Both, if necessary, I presume. What are your politics?

JACK   Well, I am afraid I really have none. I am a Liberal Unionist.

LADY B.   Oh, they count as Tories. They dine with us. Or come in the evening, at any rate. Now to minor matters. Are your parents living?

JACK   I have lost both my parents.

LADY B.   To lose one parent, Mr Worthing, may be regarded as a misfortune; to lose both looks like carelessness. Who was your father? He was evidently a man of some wealth. Was he born in what the Radical papers call the purple of commerce, or did he rise from the ranks of aristocracy?

JACK   I am afraid I really don't know. The fact is, Lady Bracknell, I said I had lost my parents. It would be nearer the truth to say that my parents seem to have lost me ... I don't actually know who I am by birth. I was ... well, I was found.

LADY B.   Found!

JACK   The late Mr Thomas Cardew, an old gentleman of a very charitable and kindly disposition, found me, and gave me the name of Worthing, because he happened to have a first-class ticket for Worthing in his pocket at the time. Worthing is a place in Sussex. It is a seaside resort.

LADY B.   Where did the charitable gentleman who had a first-class ticket for this seaside resort find you?

JACK   (*gravely*) In a handbag.

LADY B.   A handbag?

JACK   (*very seriously*) Yes, Lady Bracknell. I was in a handbag – a somewhat large, black leather handbag, with handles to it – an ordinary handbag, in fact.

LADY B.   In what locality did this Mr James, or Thomas, Cardew come across this ordinary handbag?

JACK   In the cloak room at Victoria Station. It was given to him in mistake for his own.

LADY B.   The cloak room at Victoria Station?

JACK   Yes. The Brighton line.

LADY B.   The line is immaterial. Mr Worthing, I confess I feel somewhat bewildered by what you have just told me. To be born, or at any rate, bred in a handbag, whether it had handles or not, seems to me to display a contempt for the ordinary decencies of family life that reminds one of the worst excesses of the French Revolution. And I presume you know what that unfortunate movement led to? As for the particular locality in which the handbag was found, a cloakroom at a railway station might serve to conceal a social indiscretion – has probably, indeed, been used for that purpose before now – but it could hardly be regarded as an assured basis for a recognized position in good society.

JACK   May I ask you then what you would advise me to do? I need hardly say I would do anything in the world to ensure Gwendolen's happiness.

LADY B.   I would strongly advise you, Mr Worthing, to try and acquire some relations as soon as possible, and to make a definite effort to produce at any rate one parent, of either sex, before the season is quite over.

JACK   Well, I don't see how I could possibly manage to do that. I can produce the handbag at any moment. It is in my dressing room at home. I really think that should satisfy you, Lady Bracknell.

LADY B.   Me, sir! What has it to do with me? You can hardly imagine that I and Lord Bracknell would dream of allowing our only daughter – a girl brought up with the utmost care – to marry into a cloakroom, and form an alliance with a parcel? Good morning, Mr Worthing! (LADY BRACKNELL *sweeps out in majestic indignation.*)

JACK   Good morning! (ALGERNON, *from the other room, strikes up the Wedding March.* JACK *looks perfectly furious, and goes to the door.*) For goodness' sake don't play that ghastly tune,

Algy! How idiotic you are! (*The music stops, and* ALGERNON *enters cheerily.*)

ALGERNON Didn't it go off all right, old boy? You don't mean to say Gwendolen refused you? I know it is a way she has. She is always refusing people. I think it is most ill-natured of her.

JACK Oh, Gwendolen is as right as a trivet. As far as she is concerned, we are engaged. Her mother is perfectly unbearable. Never met such a Gorgon ... I don't really know what a Gorgon is like, but I am quite sure that Lady Bracknell is one. In any case, she is a monster, without being a myth, which is rather unfair ... I beg your pardon, Algy, I suppose I shouldn't talk about your own aunt in that way before you.

ALGERNON My dear boy, I love hearing my relations abused. It is the only thing that makes me put up with them at all. Relations are simply a tedious pack of people who haven't got the remotest knowledge of how to live, nor the smallest instinct about when to die.

JACK Oh, that is nonsense!

ALGERNON It isn't!

JACK Well, I won't argue about the matter. You always want to argue about things.

ALGERNON That is exactly what things were originally made for.

JACK Upon my word, if I thought that, I'd shoot myself ... (*A pause.*) You don't think there is any chance of Gwendolen becoming like her mother in about a hundred and fifty years, do you, Algy?

ALGERNON All women become like their mothers. That is their tragedy. No man does. That's his.

JACK Is that clever?

ALGERNON It is perfectly phrased and quite as true as any observation in civilized life should be.

JACK I am sick to death of cleverness. Everybody is clever nowadays. You can't go anywhere without meeting clever people. The thing has become an absolute public nuisance. I wish to goodness we had a few fools left.

ALGERNON We have.

JACK I should extremely like to meet them. What do they talk about?

ALGERNON The fools? Oh! about the clever people, of course.

JACK What fools!

ALGERNON By the way, did you tell Gwendolen the truth about your being Ernest in town, and Jack in the country?

JACK (*in a very patronizing manner*) My dear fellow, the truth isn't quite the sort of thing one tells to a nice sweet refined girl. What extraordinary ideas you have about the way to behave to a woman!

ALGERNON The only way to behave to a woman is to make love to her, if she is pretty, and to someone else if she is plain.

JACK Oh, that is nonsense.

ALGERNON What about your brother? What about the profligate Ernest?

JACK Oh, before the end of the week I shall have got rid of him. I'll say he died in Paris of apoplexy. Lots of people die of apoplexy, quite suddenly, don't they?

ALGERNON Yes, but it's hereditary, my dear fellow. It's a sort of thing that runs in families. You had much better say a severe chill.

JACK You are sure a severe chill isn't hereditary, or anything of that kind?

ALGERNON Of course it isn't!

JACK Very well, then. My poor brother Ernest is carried off suddenly in Paris, by a severe chill. That gets rid of him.

ALGERNON But I thought you said that ... Miss Cardew was a little too much interested in your poor brother Ernest? Won't she feel his loss a good deal?

JACK Oh, that is all right. Cecily is not a silly romantic girl, I am glad to say. She has got a capital appetite, goes long walks, and pays no attention at all to her lessons.

ALGERNON I would rather like to see Cecily.

JACK I will take very good care you never do. She is excessively pretty, and she is only just eighteen.

ALGERNON Have you told Gwendolen yet that you have an excessively pretty ward who is only just eighteen?

JACK Oh! one doesn't blurt these things out to people. Cecily and Gwendolen are perfectly certain to be extremely great friends. I'll bet you anything you like that half an hour after they have met, they will be calling each other sister.

ALGERNON Women only do that when they have called each other a lot of other things first. Now, my dear boy, if we want to get a good table at Willis's, we really must go and dress. Do you know it is nearly seven?

JACK (*irritably*) Oh! it always is nearly seven.

ALGERNON Well, I'm hungry.

JACK I never knew you when you weren't... .

ALGERNON What shall we do after dinner? Go to the theatre?

JACK Oh no! I loathe listening.

ALGERNON Well, let us go to the club?

JACK Oh, no! I hate talking.

ALGERNON Well, we might trot round to the Empire at ten?

JACK Oh no! I can't bear looking at things. It is so silly.

ALGERNON Well, what shall we do?

JACK Nothing!

ALGERNON It is awfully hard work doing nothing. However I don't mind hard work where there is no definite object of any kind. (*Enter* LANE.)

LANE Miss Fairfax. (*Enter* GWENDOLEN. LANE *goes out*.)

ALGERNON Gwendolen, upon my word!

GWENDOLEN Algy, kindly turn your back. I have something very particular to say to Mr Worthing.

ALGERNON Really, Gwendolen, I don't think I can allow this at all.

GWENDOLEN Algy, you always adopt a strictly immoral attitude towards life. You are not quite old enough to do that. (ALGERNON *retires to the fireplace*.)

JACK My own darling!

GWENDOLEN Ernest, we may never be married. From the expression on mamma's face I fear we never shall. Few parents nowadays pay any regard to what their children say to them. The old-fashioned respect for the young is fast dying out. Whatever influence I ever had over mamma, I lost at the age of three. But although she may prevent us from becoming man and wife, and I may marry someone else, and marry often, nothing that she can possibly do can alter my eternal devotion to you.

JACK Dear Gwendolen!

GWENDOLEN The story of your romantic origin, as related to me by mamma, with unpleasing comments, has naturally stirred the deeper fibres of my nature. Your Christian name has an irresistible fascination. The simplicity of your character makes you exquisitely incomprehensible to me. Your town address at the Albany I have. What is your address in the country?

JACK The Manor House, Woolton, Hertfordshire. (ALGERNON, *who has been carefully listening, smiles to himself, and writes the address on his shirtcuff. Then picks up the 'Railway Guide'.*)

GWENDOLEN There is a good postal service, I suppose? It may be necessary to do something desperate. That of course will require serious consideration. I will communicate with you daily.

JACK My own one!

GWENDOLEN How long do you remain in town?

JACK   Till Monday.

GWENDOLEN   Good! Algy, you may turn round now.

ALGERNON   Thanks, I've turned round already.

GWENDOLEN   You may also ring the bell.

JACK   You will let me see you to your carriage, my own darling?

GWENDOLEN   Certainly.

JACK   (*to* LANE, *who now enters*) I will see Miss Fairfax out.

LANE   Yes, sir. (JACK *and* GWENDOLEN *go off.* LANE *presents several letters on a salver to* ALGERNON. *It is to be surmised that they are bills, as* ALGERNON *after looking at the envelopes, tears them up.*)

ALGERNON   A glass of sherry, Lane.

LANE   Yes, sir.

ALGERNON   Tomorrow, Lane, I'm going Bunburying.

LANE   Yes, sir.

ALGERNON   I shall probably not be back till Monday. You can put up my dress clothes, my smoking jacket, and all the Bunbury suits ...

LANE   Yes, sir. (*Handing sherry.*)

ALGERNON   I hope tomorrow will be a fine day, Lane.

LANE   It never is, sir.

ALGERNON   Lane, you're a perfect pessimist.

LANE   I do my best to give satisfaction, sir. (*Enter* JACK. LANE *goes off.*)

JACK   There's a sensible, intellectual girl! the only girl I ever cared for in my life. (ALGERNON *is laughing immoderately.*) What on earth are you so amused at?

ALGERNON   Oh, I'm a little anxious about poor Bunbury, that is all.

JACK   If you don't take care, your friend Bunbury will get you into a serious scrape some day.

ALGERNON   I love scrapes. They are the only things that are never serious.

JACK   Oh, that's nonsense, Algy. You never talk anything but nonsense.

ALGERNON   Nobody ever does. (JACK *looks indignantly at him, and leaves the room.* ALGERNON *lights a cigarette, reads his shirtcuff, and smiles.*)

ACT-DROP

ACT TWO

The garden at the Manor House. A flight of grey stone steps leads up to the house. The garden, an old-fashioned one, full of roses. Time of year, July. Basket chairs, and a table covered with books, are set under a large yew-tree.

MISS PRISM *discovered seated at the table.* CECILY *is at the back watering flowers.*

MISS PRISM (*calling*) Cecily, Cecily! Surely such a utilitarian occupation as the watering of flowers is rather Moulton's duty than yours? Especially at a moment when intellectual pleasures await you. Your German grammar is on the table. Pray open it at page fifteen. We will repeat yesterday's lesson.

    CECILY (*coming over very slowly*) But I don't like German. It isn't at all a becoming language. I know perfectly well that I look quite plain after my German lesson.

MISS PRISM Child, you know how anxious your guardian is that you should improve yourself in every way. He laid particular stress on your German, as he was leaving for town yesterday. Indeed, he always lays stress on your German when he is leaving for town.

    CECILY Dear Uncle Jack is so very serious! Sometimes he is so serious that I think he cannot be quite well.

MISS PRISM (*drawing herself up*) Your guardian enjoys the best of health, and his gravity of demeanour is especially to be commended in one so comparatively young as he is. I know no one who has a higher sense of duty and responsibility.

    CECILY I suppose that is why he often looks a little bored when we three are together.

MISS PRISM Cecily! I am surprised at you. Mr Worthing has many troubles in his life. Idle merriment and triviality would be out of place in his conversation. You must remember his constant anxiety about that unfortunate young man, his brother.

CECILY I wish Uncle Jack would allow that unfortunate young man, his brother, to come down here sometimes. We might have a good influence over him, Miss Prism. I am sure you certainly would. You know German, and geology, and things of that kind influence a man very much. (CECILY *begins to write in her diary.*)

MISS PRISM (*shaking her head*) I do not think that even I could produce any effect on a character that according to his own brother's admission is irretrievably weak and vacillating. Indeed I am not sure that I would desire to reclaim him. I am not in favour of this modern mania for turning bad people into good people at a moment's notice. As a man sows so let him reap. You must put away your diary, Cecily. I really don't see why you should keep a diary at all.

CECILY I keep a diary in order to enter the wonderful secrets of my life. If I didn't write them down I should probably forget all about them.

MISS PRISM Memory, my dear Cecily, is the diary that we all carry about with us.

CECILY Yes, but it usually chronicles the things that have never happened, and couldn't possibly have happened. I believe that Memory is responsible for nearly all the three-volume novels that Mudie sends us.

MISS PRISM Do not speak slightingly of the three-volume novel, Cecily. I wrote one myself in earlier days.

CECILY Did you really, Miss Prism? How wonderfully clever you are. I hope it did not end happily? I don't like novels that end happily. They depress me so much.

MISS PRISM The good ended happily, and the bad unhappily. That is what Fiction means.

CECILY   I suppose so. But it seems very unfair. And was your novel ever published?

MISS PRISM   Alas! no. The manuscript unfortunately was abandoned. I use the word in the sense of lost or mislaid. To your work, child; these speculations are profitless.

CECILY   (*smiling*) But I see dear Dr Chasuble coming up through the garden.

MISS PRISM   (*rising and advancing*) Dr Chasuble! This is indeed a pleasure.

Enter CANON CHASUBLE.

CHASUBLE   And how are we this morning? Miss Prism, you are, I trust, well?

CECILY   Miss Prism has just been complaining of a slight headache. I think it would do her so much good to have a short stroll with you in the Park, Dr Chasuble.

MISS PRISM   Cecily, I have not mentioned anything about a headache.

CECILY   No, dear Miss Prism, I know that, but I felt instinctively that you had a headache. Indeed I was thinking about that, and not about my German lesson, when the Rector came in.

CHASUBLE   I hope Cecily, you are not inattentive.

CECILY   I am afraid I am.

CHASUBLE   That is strange. Were I fortunate enough to be Miss Prism's pupil, I would hang upon her lips. (MISS PRISM *glares*.) I spoke metaphorically – my metaphor was drawn from bees. Ahem! Mr Worthing I suppose, has not returned from town yet?

MISS PRISM   We do not expect him till Monday afternoon.

CHASUBLE   Ah yes, he usually likes to spend his Sunday in London. He is not one of those whose sole aim is enjoyment, as, by all accounts, that unfortunate young man his brother seems to be. But I must not disturb Egeria and her pupil any longer.

MISS PRISM   Egeria? My name is Lætitia, Doctor.

CHASUBLE (*bowing*) A classical allusion merely, drawn from the Pagan authors. I shall see you both no doubt at Evensong?

MISS PRISM I think, dear Doctor, I will have a stroll with you. I find I have a headache after all, and a walk might do it good.

CHASUBLE With pleasure, Miss Prism, with pleasure. We might go as far as the schools and back.

MISS PRISM That would be delightful. Cecily, you will read your Political Economy in my absence. The chapter on the Fall of the Rupee you may omit. It is somewhat too sensational. Even these metallic problems have their melodramatic side. (*Goes down the garden with* DR CHASUBLE.)

CECILY (*picks up books and throws them back on table*) Horrid Political Economy! Horrid Geography! Horrid, horrid German! (*Enter* MERRIMAN *with a card on a salver.*)

MERRIMAN Mr Ernest Worthing has just driven over from the station. He has brought his luggage with him.

CECILY (*takes the card and reads it*) 'Mr Ernest Worthing, B. 4, The Albany, W.' Uncle Jack's brother! Did you tell him Mr Worthing was in town?

MERRIMAN Yes, Miss. He seemed very much disappointed. I mentioned that you and Miss Prism were in the garden. He said he was anxious to speak to you privately for a moment.

CECILY Ask Mr Ernest Worthing to come here. I suppose you had better talk to the housekeeper about a room for him.

MERRIMAN Yes, Miss. (MERRIMAN *goes off.*)

CECILY I have never met any really wicked person before. I feel rather frightened. I am so afraid he will look just like everyone else. (*Enter* ALGERNON, *very gay and debonair.*) He does!

ALGERNON (*raising his hat*) You are my little cousin Cecily, I'm sure.

CECILY   You are under some strange mistake. I am not little. In fact, I believe I am more than usually tall for my age. (ALGERNON *is rather taken aback.*) But I am your cousin Cecily. You, I see from your card, are Uncle Jack's brother, my cousin Ernest, my wicked cousin Ernest.

ALGERNON Oh! I am not really wicked at all, cousin Cecily. You mustn't think that I am wicked.

CECILY   If you are not, then you have certainly been deceiving us all in a very inexcusable manner. I hope you have not been leading a double life, pretending to be wicked and being really good all the time. That would be hypocrisy.

ALGERNON (*looks at her in amazement*) Oh! Of course I have been rather reckless.

CECILY   I am glad to hear it.

ALGERNON In fact, now you mention the subject, I have been very bad in my own small way.

CECILY   I don't think you should be so proud of that, though I am sure it must have been very pleasant.

ALGERNON It is much pleasanter being here with you.

CECILY   I can't understand how you are here at all. Uncle Jack won't be back till Monday afternoon.

ALGERNON That is a great disappointment. I am obliged to go up by the first train on Monday morning. I have a business appointment that I am anxious ... to miss.

CECILY   Couldn't you miss it anywhere but in London?

ALGERNON No: the appointment is in London.

CECILY   Well, I know, of course, how important it is not to keep a business engagement, if one wants to retain any sense of the beauty of life, but still I think you had better wait till Uncle Jack arrives. I know he wants to speak to you about your emigrating.

ALGERNON About my what?

CECILY   Your emigrating. He has gone up to buy your outfit.

ALGERNON I certainly wouldn't let Jack buy my outfit. He has no taste in neckties at all.

CECILY   I don't think you will require neckties. Uncle Jack is sending you to Australia.

ALGERNON   Australia? I'd sooner die.

CECILY   Well, he said at dinner on Wednesday night, that you would have to choose between this world, the next world, and Australia.

ALGERNON   Oh, well! The accounts I have received of Australia and the next world are not particularly encouraging. This world is good enough for me, cousin Cecily.

CECILY   Yes, but are you good enough for it?

ALGERNON   I'm afraid I'm not that. That is why I want you to reform me. You might make that your mission, if you don't mind, cousin Cecily.

CECILY   I'm afraid I've no time, this afternoon.

ALGERNON   Well, would you mind my reforming myself this afternoon?

CECILY   It is rather Quixotic of you. But I think you should try.

ALGERNON   I will. I feel better already.

CECILY   You are looking a little worse.

ALGERNON   That is because I am hungry.

CECILY   How thoughtless of me. I should have remembered that when one is going to lead an entirely new life, one requires regular and wholesome meals. Won't you come in?

ALGERNON   Thank you. Might I have a buttonhole first? I never have any appetite unless I have a buttonhole first.

CECILY   A Maréchale Niel? (*Picks up scissors.*)

ALGERNON   No, I'd sooner have a pink rose.

CECILY   Why? (*Cuts a flower.*)

ALGERNON   Because you are like a pink rose, cousin Cecily.

CECILY   I don't think it can be right for you to talk to me like that. Miss Prism never says such things to me.

ALGERNON   Then Miss Prism is a short-sighted old lady. (CECILY *puts the rose in his buttonhole.*) You are the prettiest girl I ever saw.

CECILY   Miss Prism says that all good looks are a snare.

ALGERNON   They are a snare that every sensible man would like
          to be caught in.

CECILY   Oh! I don't think I would care to catch a sensible
          man. I shouldn't know what to talk to him about.
          (*They pass into the house.* MISS PRISM *and* DR CHASUBLE
          return.)

MISS PRISM You are too much alone, dear Dr Chasuble. You
          should get married. A misanthrope I can understand
          – a womanthrope, never!

CHASUBLE   (*with a scholar's shudder*) Believe me, I do not
          deserve so neologistic a phrase. The precept as well
          as the practice of the Primitive Church was distinctly
          against matrimony.

MISS PRISM (*sententiously*) That is obviously the reason why the
          Primitive Church has not lasted up to the present
          day. And you do not seem to realize, dear Doctor,
          that by persistently remaining single, a man converts
          himself into a permanent public temptation. Men
          should be more careful; this very celibacy leads
          weaker vessels astray.

CHASUBLE   But is a man not equally attractive when married?

MISS PRISM No married man is ever attractive except to his wife.

CHASUBLE   And often, I've been told, not even to her.

MISS PRISM That depends on the intellectual sympathies of the
          woman. Maturity can always be depended on.
          Ripeness can be trusted. Young women are green.
          (DR CHASUBLE *starts.*) I spoke horticulturally. My
          metaphor was drawn from fruits. But where is Cecily?

CHASUBLE   Perhaps she followed us to the schools. (*Enter* JACK
          *slowly from the back of the garden. He is dressed in
          the deepest mourning, with crêpe hatband and black
          gloves.*)

MISS PRISM Mr Worthing!

CHASUBLE   Mr Worthing?

MISS PRISM This is indeed a surprise. We did not look for you
          till Monday afternoon.

JACK (*shakes* MISS PRISM'S *hand in a tragic manner*) I have returned sooner than I expected. Dr Chasuble, I hope you are well?

CHASUBLE Dear Mr Worthing. I trust this garb of woe does not betoken some terrible calamity?

JACK My brother.

MISS PRISM More shameful debts and extravagance?

CHASUBLE Still leading his life of pleasure?

JACK (*shaking his head*) Dead!

CHASUBLE Your brother Ernest dead?

JACK Quite dead.

MISS PRISM What a lesson for him! I trust he will profit by it.

CHASUBLE Mr Worthing, I offer you my sincere condolence. You have at least the consolation of knowing that you were always the most generous and forgiving of brothers.

JACK Poor Ernest! He had many faults, but it is a sad, sad blow.

CHASUBLE Very sad indeed. Were you with him at the end?

JACK No. He died abroad; in Paris, in fact. I had a telegram last night from the manager of the Grand Hotel.

CHASUBLE Was the cause of death mentioned?

JACK A severe chill, it seems.

MISS PRISM As a man sows, so shall he reap.

CHASUBLE (*raising his hand*) Charity, dear Miss Prism, charity! None of us are perfect. I myself am peculiarly susceptible to draughts. Will the internment take place here?

JACK No. He seemed to have expressed a desire to be buried in Paris.

CHASUBLE In Paris! (*Shakes his head.*) I fear that hardly points to any very serious state of mind at the last. You would no doubt wish me to make some slight allusion to this tragic domestic affliction next Sunday. (JACK *presses his hand convulsively.*) My sermon on the meaning of the manna in the wilderness can be adapted to almost any occasion, joyful, or, as in the present case, distressing. (*All sigh.*) I have preached it at harvest celebrations, christenings, confirmations, on days of humiliation and festal days. The last time I delivered it was in the Cathedral, as a charity sermon on behalf of the Society for the Prevention of Discontent among the Upper Orders. The Bishop, who was present, was much struck by some of the analogies I drew.

JACK Ah! that reminds me, you mentioned christenings, I think, Dr Chasuble? I suppose you know how to christen all right? (DR CHASUBLE *looks astounded.*) I mean, of course, you are continually christening, aren't you?

MISS PRISM It is, I regret to say, one of the Rector's most constant duties in this parish. I have often spoken to the poorer classes on the subject. But they don't seem to know what thrift is.

CHASUBLE But is there any particular infant in whom you are interested, Mr Worthing? Your brother was, I believe, unmarried, was he not.

JACK Oh yes.

MISS PRISM (*bitterly*) People who live entirely for pleasure usually are.

JACK But it is not for any child, dear Doctor. I am very fond of children. No! the fact is, I would like to be christened myself, this afternoon, if you have nothing better to do.

CHASUBLE But surely, Mr Worthing, you have been christened already?

JACK I don't remember anything about it.

CHASUBLE But have you any grave doubts on the subject?

JACK I certainly intend to have. Of course I don't know if the thing would bother you in any way, or if you think I am a little too old now.

CHASUBLE Not at all. The sprinkling, and, indeed, the immersion of adults is a perfectly canonical practice.

JACK Immersion!

CHASUBLE   You need have no apprehensions. Sprinkling is all
            that is necessary, or indeed I think advisable. Our
            weather is so changeable. And what hour would you
            wish the ceremony performed?

JACK   Oh, I might trot round about five if that would suit
            you.

CHASUBLE   Perfectly, perfectly! In fact I have two similar
            ceremonies to perform at that time. A case of twins
            that occurred recently in one of the outlying cottages
            on your own estate. Poor Jenkins the carter, a most
            hard-working man.

JACK   Oh! I don't see much fun in being christened along
            with other babies. It would be childish. Would half
            past five do?

CHASUBLE   Admirably! Admirably! (*Takes out watch.*) And now,
            dear Mr Worthing, I will not intrude any longer into a
            house of sorrow. I would merely beg you not to be
            too much bowed down by grief. What seem to us
            bitter trials are often blessings in disguise.

MISS PRISM This seems to me a blessing of an extremely obvious
            kind. (*Enter* CECILY *from the house.*)

CECILY   Uncle Jack! Oh, I am pleased to see you back. But
            what horrid clothes you have got on! Do go and
            change them.

MISS PRISM Cecily!

CHASUBLE   My child! my child! (CECILY *goes towards* JACK; *he kisses
            her brow in a melancholy manner.*)

CECILY   What is the matter, Uncle Jack? Do look happy! You
            look as if you had toothache, and I have got such a
            surprise for you. Who do you think is in the dining-
            room? Your brother!

JACK   Who?

CECILY   Your brother Ernest. He arrived about half an hour
            ago.

JACK   What nonsense! I haven't got a brother!

CECILY Oh, don't say that. However badly he may have
behaved to you in the past he is still your brother.
You couldn't be so heartless as to disown him. I'll tell
him to come out. And you will shake hands with him,
won't you, Uncle Jack? (*Runs back into the house.*)

CHASUBLE These are very joyful tidings.

MISS PRISM After we had all been resigned to his loss, his sudden
return seems to me peculiarly distressing.

JACK My brother is in the dining-room? I don't know what
it all means. I think it is perfectly absurd. (*Enter*
ALGERNON *and* CECILY *hand in hand. They come slowly
up to* JACK.)

JACK Good heavens! (*Motions* ALGERNON *away.*)

ALGERNON Brother John, I have come down from town to tell
you that I am very sorry for all the trouble I have
given you, and that I intend to lead a better life in the
future. (JACK *glares at him and does not take his
hand.*)

CECILY Uncle Jack, you are not going to refuse your own
brother's hand?

JACK Nothing will induce me to take his hand. I think his
coming down here disgraceful. He knows perfectly
well why.

CECILY Uncle Jack, do be nice. There is some good in
everyone. Ernest has just been telling me about his
poor invalid friend Mr Bunbury whom he goes to visit
so often. And surely there must be much good in one
who is kind to an invalid, and leaves the pleasures of
London to sit by a bed of pain.

JACK Oh! he has been talking about Bunbury, has he?

CECILY Yes, he has told me all about poor Mr Bunbury, and
his terrible state of health.

JACK Bunbury! Well, I won't have him talk to you about
Bunbury or about anything else. It is enough to drive
one perfectly frantic.

ALGERNON Of course I admit that the faults were all on my side.
But I must say that I think that Brother John's coldness to me is peculiarly painful. I expected a more

enthusiastic welcome, especially considering it is the first time I have come here.

CECILY Uncle Jack, if you don't shake hands with Ernest, I will never forgive you.

JACK Never forgive me?

CECILY Never, never, never!

JACK Well, this is the last time I shall ever do it. (*Shakes hands with* ALGERNON *and glares.*)

CHASUBLE It's pleasant, is it not, to see so perfect a reconciliation? I think we might leave the two brothers together.

MISS PRISM Cecily, you will come with us.

CECILY Certainly, Miss Prism. My little task of reconciliation is over.

CHASUBLE You have done a beautiful action to-day, dear child.

MISS PRISM We must not be premature in our judgements.

CECILY I feel very happy. (*They all go off.*)

JACK You young scoundrel, Algy, you must get out of this place as soon as possible. I don't allow any Bunburying here. (*Enter* MERRIMAN.)

MERRIMAN I have put Mr Ernest's things in the room next to yours, sir. I suppose that is all right?

JACK What?

MERRIMAN Mr Ernest's luggage, sir. I have unpacked it and put it in the room next to your own.

JACK His luggage?

MERRIMAN Yes, sir. Three portmanteaus, a dressing-case, two hat boxes, and a large luncheon-basket.

ALGERNON I am afraid I can't stay more than a week this time.

JACK Merriman, order the dog-cart at once. Mr Ernest has been suddenly called back to town.

MERRIMAN Yes, sir. (*Goes back into the house.*)

ALGERNON What a fearful liar you are, Jack. I have not been called back to town at all.

JACK Yes, you have.

ALGERNON I haven't heard anyone call me.

JACK Your duty as a gentleman calls you back.

ALGERNON My duty as a gentleman has never interfered with my pleasures in the smallest degree.

JACK I can quite understand that.

ALGERNON Well, Cecily is a darling.

JACK You are not to talk of Miss Cardew like that. I don't like it.

ALGERNON Well, I don't like your clothes. You look perfectly ridiculous in them. Why on earth don't you go up and change? It is perfectly childish to be in deep mourning for a man who is actually staying for a whole week with you in your house as a guest. I call it grotesque.

JACK You are certainly not staying with me for a whole week as a guest or anything else. You have got to leave ... by the four-five train.

ALGERNON I certainly won't leave you so long as you are in mourning. It would be most unfriendly. If I were in mourning you would stay with me, I suppose. I should think it very unkind if you didn't.

JACK Well, will you go if I change my clothes?

ALGERNON Yes, if you are not too long. I never saw anybody take so long to dress, and with such little result.

JACK Well, at any rate, that is better than being always over-dressed as you are.

ALGERNON If I am occasionally a little over-dressed, I make up for it by being always immensely over-educated.

JACK Your vanity is ridiculous, your conduct an outrage, and your presence in my garden utterly absurd. However, you have got to catch the four-five, and I hope you will have a pleasant journey back to town. This Bunburying, as you call it, has not been a great success for you. (*Goes into the house.*)

ALGERNON I think it has been a great success. I'm in love with Cecily, and that is everything. (*Enter* CECILY *at the*

*back of the garden. She picks up the can and begins
to water the flowers.*) But I must see her before I go,
and make arrangements for another Bunbury. Ah,
there she is.

CECILY   Oh, I merely came back to water the roses. I thought
you were with Uncle Jack.

ALGERNON   He's gone to order the dog-cart for me.

CECILY   Oh, is he going to take you for a nice drive?

ALGERNON   He's going to send me away.

CECILY   Then have we got to part?

ALGERNON   I am afraid so. It's very painful parting.

CECILY   It is always painful to part from people whom one
has known for a very brief space of time. The
absence of old friends one can endure with
equanimity. But even a momentary separation from
anyone to whom one has just been introduced is
almost unbearable.

ALGERNON   Thank you. (*Enter* MERRIMAN.)

MERRIMAN   The dog-cart is at the door, sir. (ALGERNON *looks
appealingly at* CECILY.)

CECILY   It can wait, Merriman ... for ... five minute.

MERRIMAN   Yes, Miss. (*Exit* MERRIMAN.)

ALGERNON   I hope, Cecily, I shall not offend you if I state quite
frankly and openly that you seem to me to be in
every way the visible personification of absolute
perfection.

CECILY   I think your frankness does you great credit, Ernest. If
you will allow me I will copy your remarks into my
diary. (*Goes over to table and begins writing in diary.*)

ALGERNON   Do you really keep a diary? I'd give anything to look
at it. May I?

CECILY   Oh no. (*Puts her hand over it.*) You see, it is simply a
very young girl's record of her own thoughts and
impressions, and consequently meant for publication.
When it appears in volume form I hope you will
order a copy. But pray, Ernest, don't stop. I delight
in taking down from dictation. I have reached
'absolute perfection'. You can go on. I am quite
ready for more.

ALGERNON (*somewhat taken aback*) Ahem! Ahem!

CECILY Oh, don't cough, Ernest. When one is dictating one should speak fluently and not cough. Besides, I don't know how to spell a cough. (*Writes as* ALGERNON *speaks.*)

ALGERNON (*speaking very rapidly*) Cecily, ever since I first looked upon your wonderful and incomparable beauty, I have dared to love you wildly, passionately, devotedly, hopelessly.

CECILY I don't think that you should tell me that you love me wildly, passionately, devotedly, hopelessly. Hopelessly doesn't seem to make much sense, does it?

ALGERNON Cecily! (*Enter* MERRIMAN.)

MERRIMAN The dog-cart is waiting, sir.

ALGERNON Tell it to come round next week, at the same hour.

MERRIMAN (*looks at* CECILY, *who makes no sign*) Yes, sir. (MERRIMAN *retires.*)

CECILY Uncle Jack would be very much annoyed if he knew you were staying on till next week, at the same hour.

ALGERNON Oh, I don't care about Jack. I don't care for anybody in the whole world but you. I love you, Cecily. You will marry me, won't you.

CECILY You silly boy! Of course. Why, we have been engaged for the last three months.

ALGERNON For the last three months?

CECILY Yes, it will be exactly three months on Thursday.

ALGERNON But how did we become engaged?

CECILY Well, ever since dear Uncle Jack first confessed to us that he had a younger brother who was very wicked and bad, you of course have formed the chief topic of conversation between myself and Miss Prism. And of course a man who is much talked about is always very attractive. One feels there must be something in him after all. I daresay it was foolish of me, but I fell in love with you, Ernest.

ALGERNON   Darling! And when was the engagement actually settled?

CECILY   On the 14th of February last. Worn out by your entire ignorance of my existence, I determined to end the matter one way or the other, and after a long struggle with myself I accepted you under this dear old tree here. The next day I bought this little ring in your name, and this is the little bangle with the true lovers' knot I promised you always to wear.

ALGERNON   Did I give you this? It's very pretty, isn't it?

CECILY   Yes, you've wonderfully good taste, Ernest. It's the excuse I've always given for your leading such a bad life. And this is the box in which I keep all your dear letters. (*Kneels at table, opens box, and produces letters tied up with blue ribbon.*)

ALGERNON   My letters! But my own sweet Cecily, I have never written you any letters.

CECILY   You need hardly remind me of that, Ernest. I remember only too well that I was forced to write your letters for you. I always wrote three times a week, and sometimes oftener.

ALGERNON   Oh, do let me read them, Cecily!

CECILY   Oh, I couldn't possibly. They would make you far too conceited. (*Replaces box.*) The three you wrote me after I had broken off the engagement are so beautiful, and so badly spelled, that even now I can hardly read them without crying a little.

ALGERNON   But was our engagement ever broken off?

CECILY   Of course it was. On the 22nd of last March. You can see the entry if you like. (*Shows diary.*) 'Today I broke off my engagement with Ernest. I feel it is better to do so. The weather still continues charming.'

ALGERNON   But why on earth did you break it off? What had I done? I had done nothing at all. Cecily, I am very much hurt indeed to hear you broke it off. Particularly when the weather was so charming.

CECILY   It would hardly have been a really serious
          engagement if it hadn't been broken off at least
          once. But I forgave you before the week was out.

ALGERNON (*crossing to her, and kneeling*) What a perfect angel
          you are, Cecily.

CECILY   You dear romantic boy. (*He kisses her, she puts her
          fingers through his hair.*) I hope your hair curls
          naturally, does it?

ALGERNON Yes, darling, with a little help from others.

CECILY   I am so glad.

ALGERNON You'll never break off our engagement again,
          Cecily?

CECILY   I don't think I could break it off now that I have
          actually met you. Besides, of course, there is the
          question of your name.

ALGERNON Yes, of course. (*Nervously.*)

CECILY   You must not laugh at me, darling, but it had
          always been a girlish dream of mine to love
          someone whose name was Ernest. (ALGERNON *rises,
          CECILY also.*) There is something in that name that
          seems to inspire absolute confidence. I pity any
          poor married woman whose husband is not called
          Ernest.

ALGERNON But, my dear child, do you mean to say you could
          not love me if I had some other name?

CECILY   But what name?

ALGERNON Oh, any name you like – Algernon – for instance ...

CECILY   But I don't like the name of Algernon.

ALGERNON Well, my own dear, sweet, loving little darling, I
          really can't see why you should object to the name
          of Algernon. It is not at all a bad name. In fact, it is
          rather an aristocratic name. Half of the chaps who
          get into the Bankruptcy Court are called Algernon.
          But seriously, Cecily ... (*Moving to her*) if my name
          was Algy, couldn't you love me?

CECILY   I might respect you, Ernest, I might admire your character, but I fear that I should not be able to give you my undivided attention.

ALGERNON   Ahem! Cecily! (*Picking up hat.*) Your Rector here is, I suppose, thoroughly experienced in the practice of all the rites and ceremonials of the Church?

CECILY   Oh, yes. Dr Chasuble is a most learned man. He has never written a single book, so you can imagine how much he knows.

ALGERNON   I must see him at once on a most important christening – I mean on most important business.

CECILY   Oh!

ALGERNON   I shan't be away more than half an hour.

CECILY   Considering that we have been engaged since February the 14th, and that I only met you today for the first time, I think it is rather hard that you should leave me for so long a period as half an hour. Couldn't you make it twenty minutes?

ALGERNON   I'll be back in no time. (*Kisses her and rushes down the garden.*)

CECILY   What an impetuous boy he is! I like his hair so much. I must enter his proposal in my diary. (*Enter* MERRIMAN.)

MERRIMAN   A Miss Fairfax has just called to see Mr Worthing. On very important business Miss Fairfax states.

CECILY   Isn't Mr Worthing in his library?

MERRIMAN   Mr Worthing went over in the direction of the Rectory some time ago.

CECILY   Pray ask the lady to come out here; Mr Worthing is sure to be back soon. And you can bring tea.

MERRIMAN   Yes, Miss. (*Goes out.*)

CECILY   Miss Fairfax! I suppose one of the many good elderly women who are associated with Uncle Jack in some of his philanthropic work in London. I don't quite like women who are interested in philanthropic work. I think it is so forward of them. (*Enter* MERRIMAN.)

MERRIMAN   Miss Fairfax. (*Enter* GWENDOLEN.) (*Exit* MERRIMAN.)

CECILY   (*advancing to meet her*) Pray let me introduce myself to you. My name is Cecily Cardew.

GWENDOLEN   Cecily Cardew? (*Moving to her and shaking hands*) What a very sweet name! Something tells me that we are going to be great friends. I like you already more than I can say. My first impressions of people are never wrong.

CECILY   How nice of you to like me so much after we have known each other such a comparatively short time. Pray sit down.

GWENDOLEN   (*still standing up*) I may call you Cecily, may I not?

CECILY   With pleasure!

GWENDOLEN   And you will always call me Gwendolen, won't you?

CECILY   If you wish.

GWENDOLEN   Then that is all quite settled, is it not?

CECILY   I hope so. (*A pause. They both sit down together.*)

GWENDOLEN   Perhaps this might be a favourable opportunity for my mentioning who I am. My father is Lord Bracknell. You have never heard of papa, I suppose?

CECILY   I don't think so.

GWENDOLEN   Outside the family circle, papa, I am glad to say, is entirely unknown. I think that is quite as it should be. The home seems to me to be the proper sphere for the man. And certainly once a man begins to neglect his domestic duties he becomes painfully effeminate, does he not? And I don't like that. It makes men so very attractive. Cecily, mamma, whose views on education are remarkably strict, has brought me up to be extremely short-sighted; it is part of her system; so do you mind my looking at you through my glasses?

CECILY   Oh! not at all, Gwendolen. I am very fond of being looked at.

GWENDOLEN (*after examining* CECILY *carefully through a lorgnette*)
You are here on a short visit I suppose.

CECILY Oh no! I live here.

GWENDOLEN (*severely*) Really? Your mother, no doubt, or some
female relative of advanced years, resides here also?

CECILY Oh no! I have no mother, nor, in fact, any relations.

GWENDOLEN Indeed?

CECILY My dear guardian, with the assistance of Miss Prism,
has the arduous task of looking after me.

GWENDOLEN Your guardian?

CECILY Yes, I am Mr Worthing's ward.

GWENDOLEN Oh! It is strange he never mentioned to me that he
had a ward. How secretive of him! He grows more
interesting hourly. I am not sure, however, that the
news inspires me with feelings of unmixed delight.
(*Rising and going to her.*) I am very fond of you,
Cecily; I have liked you ever since I met you! But I
am bound to state that now that I know that you are
Mr Worthing's ward, I cannot help expressing a wish
you were – well just a little older than you seem to
be – and not quite so very alluring in appearance. In
fact, if I may speak candidly —

CECILY Pray do! I think that whenever one has anything
unpleasant to say, one should always be quite
candid.

GWENDOLEN Well, to speak with perfect candour, Cecily, I wish
that you were fully forty-two, and more than usually
plain for your age. Ernest has a strong upright
nature. He is the very soul of truth and honour.
Disloyalty would be as impossible to him as
deception. But even men of the noblest possible
moral character are extremely susceptible to the
influence of the physical charms of others. Modern,
no less than Ancient History, supplies us with many
most painful examples of what I refer to. If it were
not so, indeed, History would be quite unreadable.

CECILY I beg your pardon, Gwendolen, did you say Ernest?

GWENDOLEN Yes.

CECILY   Oh, but it is not Mr Ernest Worthing who is my guardian. It is his brother – his elder brother.

GWENDOLEN   (*sitting down again*) Ernest never mentioned to me that he had a brother.

CECILY   I am sorry to say they have not been on good terms for a long time.

GWENDOLEN   Ah! that accounts for it. And now that I think of it I have never heard any man mention his brother. The subject seems distasteful to most men. Cecily, you have lifted a load from my mind. I was growing almost anxious. It would have been terrible if any cloud had come across a friendship like ours, would it not? Of course you are quite, quite sure that it is not Mr Ernest Worthing who is your guardian?

CECILY   Quite sure. (*A pause.*) In fact, I am going to be his.

GWENDOLEN   (*enquiringly*) I beg your pardon?

CECILY   (*rather shy and confidingly*) Dearest Gwendolen, there is no reason why I should make a secret of it to you. Our little county newspaper is sure to chronicle the fact next week. Mr Ernest Worthing and I are engaged to be married.

GWENDOLEN   (*quite politely, rising*) My darling Cecily, I think there must be some slight error. Mr Ernest Worthing is engaged to me. The announcement will appear in the *Morning Post* on Saturday at the latest.

CECILY   (*very politely, rising*) I am afraid you must be under some misconception. Ernest proposed to me exactly ten minutes ago. (*Shows diary.*)

GWENDOLEN   (*examines diary through her lorgnette carefully*) It is certainly very curious, for he asked me to be his wife yesterday afternoon at 5.30. If you would care to verify the incident, pray do so. (*Produces diary of her own.*) I never travel without my diary. One should always have something sensational to read in the train. I am so sorry, dear Cecily, if it is any disappointment to you, but I am afraid I have the prior claim.

CECILY   It would distress me more than I can tell you, dear
          Gwendolen, if it caused you any mental or physical
          anguish, but I feel bound to point out that since
          Ernest proposed to you he clearly has changed his
          mind.

GWENDOLEN (*meditatively*) If the poor fellow has been entrapped
          into any foolish promise I shall consider it my duty to
          rescue him at once, and with a firm hand.

CECILY   (*thoughtfully and sadly*) Whatever unfortunate
          entanglement my dear boy may have got into, I will
          never reproach him with it after we are married.

GWENDOLEN Do you allude to me, Miss Cardew, as an
          entanglement? You are presumptuous. On an
          occasion of this kind it becomes more than a moral
          duty to speak one's mind. It becomes a pleasure.

CECILY   Do you suggest, Miss Fairfax, that I entrapped Ernest
          into an engagement? How dare you? This is no time
          for wearing the shallow mask of manners. When I
          see a spade I call it a spade.

GWENDOLEN (*satirically*) I am glad to say that I have never seen a
          spade. It is obvious that our social spheres have
          been widely different. (*Enter* MERRIMAN, *followed by
          the footman. He carries a salver, table cloth, and
          plate stand.* CECILY *is about to retort. The presence of
          the servants exercises a restraining influence, under
          which both girls chafe.*)

MERRIMAN Shall I lay tea here as usual, Miss?

CECILY   (*sternly, in a calm voice*) Yes, as usual. (MERRIMAN
          begins to clear table and lay cloth. A long pause.
          CECILY *and* GWENDOLEN *glare at each other.*)

GWENDOLEN Are there many interesting walks in the vicinity, Miss
          Cardew?

CECILY   Oh! yes! a great many. From the top of one of the
          hills quite close one can see five counties.

GWENDOLEN Five counties! I don't think I should like that. I hate
          crowds.

CECILY   (*sweetly*) I suppose that is why you live in town?

GWENDOLEN *bites her lip, and beats her foot nervously with her parasol.*

GWENDOLEN (*looking round*) Quite a well-kept garden this is, Miss Cardew.

CECILY So glad you like it, Miss Fairfax.

GWENDOLEN I had no idea there were any flowers in the country.

CECILY Oh, flowers are as common here, Miss Fairfax, as people are in London.

GWENDOLEN Personally I cannot understand how anybody manages to exist in the country, if anybody who is anybody does. The country always bores me to death.

CECILY Ah! That is what the newspapers call agricultural depression, is it not? I believe the aristocracy are suffering very much from it just at present. It is almost an epidemic amongst them, I have been told. May I offer you some tea, Miss Fairfax?

GWENDOLEN (*with elaborate politeness*) Thank you. (*Aside.*) Detestable girl! But I require tea!

CECILY (*sweetly*) Sugar?

GWENDOLEN (*superciliously*) No, thank you. Sugar is not fashionable any more.

CECILY *looks angrily at her, takes up the tongs and puts four lumps of sugar into the cup.*

CECILY (*severely*) Cake or bread and butter?

GWENDOLEN (*in a bored manner*) Bread and butter, please. Cake is rarely seen at the best houses nowadays.

CECILY (*cuts a very large slice of cake, and puts it on the tray*) Hand that to Miss Fairfax. (MERRIMAN *does so, and goes out with footman.* GWENDOLEN *drinks the tea and makes a grimace. Puts down cup at once, reaches out her hand to the bread and butter, looks at it, and finds it is cake. Rises in indignation.*)

GWENDOLEN You have filled my tea with lumps of sugar, and though I asked most distinctly for bread and butter, you have given me cake. I am known for the gentleness of my disposition, and the extraordinary sweetness of my nature, but I warn you, Miss Cardew, you may go too far.

CECILY (*rising*) To save my poor, innocent, trusting boy from the machinations of any other girl there are no lengths to which I would not go.

GWENDOLEN From the moment I saw you I distrusted you. I felt that you were false and deceitful. I am never deceived in such matters. My first impressions of people are invariably right.

CECILY It seems to me, Miss Fairfax, that I am trespassing on your valuable time. No doubt you have many other calls of a similar character to make in the neighbourhood.

Enter JACK.

GWENDOLEN (*catching sight of him*) Ernest! My own Ernest!

JACK Gwendolen! Darling! (*Offers to kiss her.*)

GWENDOLEN (*drawing back*) A moment! May I ask if you are engaged to be married to this young lady? (*Points to Cecily.*)

JACK (*laughing*) To dear little Cecily! Of course not! What could have put such an idea into your pretty little head?

GWENDOLEN Thank you. You may! (*Offers her cheek.*)

CECILY (*very sweetly*) I knew there must be some mis-understanding, Miss Fairfax. The gentleman whose arm is at present round your waist is my dear guardian, Mr John Worthing.

GWENDOLEN I beg your pardon?

CECILY This is Uncle Jack.

GWENDOLEN (*receding*) Jack! Oh! (*Enter* ALGERNON.)

CECILY Here is Ernest.

ALGERNON (*goes straight over to* CECILY *without noticing anyone else*) My own love! (*Offers to kiss her.*)

CECILY (*drawing back*) A moment, Ernest! May I ask you —are you engaged to be married to this young lady?

ALGERNON (*looking round*) To what young lady? Good heavens! Gwendolen?

CECILY   Yes! to good heavens, Gwendolen, I mean to
Gwendolen.

ALGERNON   (*laughing*) Of course not! What could have put such
an idea into your pretty little head?

CECILY   Thank you. (*Presenting her cheek to be kissed.*) You
may. (ALGERNON *kisses her.*)

GWENDOLEN   I felt there was some slight error, Miss Cardew. The
gentleman who is now embracing you is my cousin,
Mr Algernon Moncrieff.

CECILY   (*breaking away from* ALGERNON) Algernon Moncrieff!
Oh! (*The two girls move towards each other and put
their arms around each other's waists as if for
protection.*)

CECILY   Are you called Algernon?

ALGERNON   I cannot deny it.

CECILY   Oh!

GWENDOLEN   Is your name really John?

JACK   (*standing rather proudly*) I could deny it if I liked. I
could deny anything if I liked. But my name
certainly is John. It has been John for years.

CECILY   (*to* GWENDOLEN) A gross deception has been
practised on both of us.

GWENDOLEN   My poor wounded Cecily!

CECILY   My sweet wronged Gwendolen!

GWENDOLEN   (*slowly and seriously*) You will call me sister, will
you not? (*They embrace.* JACK *and* ALGERNON *groan
and walk up and down.*)

CECILY   (*rather brightly*) There is just one question I would
like to ask my guardian.

GWENDOLEN   An admirable idea! Mr Worthing, there is just one
question I would like to be permitted to put to you.
Where is your brother Ernest? We are both engaged
to be married to your brother Ernest, so it is a
matter of some importance to us to know where
your brother Ernest is at present.

JACK   (*slowly and hesitatingly*) Gwendolen — Cecily — it is very painful for me to be forced to speak the truth. It is the first time in my life that I have ever been reduced to such a painful position, and I am really quite inexperienced in doing anything of the kind. However I will tell you quite frankly that I have no brother Ernest. I have no brother at all. I never had a brother in my life, and I certainly have not the smallest intention of having one in the future.

CECILY (*surprised*) No brother at all?

JACK (*cheerily*) None!

GWENDOLEN (*severely*) Had you never a brother of any kind?

JACK (*pleasantly*) Never. Not even of any kind.

GWENDOLEN I am afraid it is quite clear, Cecily, that neither of us is engaged to be married to anyone.

CECILY It is not a very pleasant position for a young girl to suddenly find herself in. Is it?

GWENDOLEN Let us go into the house. They will hardly venture to come after us there.

CECILY No, men are so cowardly, aren't they? (*They retire into the house with scornful looks.*)

JACK This ghastly state of things is what you call Bunburying, I suppose?

ALGERNON Yes, and a perfectly wonderful Bunbury it is. The most wonderful Bunbury I have ever had in my life.

JACK Well, you've no right whatsoever to Bunbury here.

ALGERNON That is absurd. One has a right to Bunbury anywhere one chooses. Every serious Bunburyist knows that.

JACK Serious Bunburyist! Good heavens!

ALGERNON Well, one must be serious about something, if one wants to have any amusement in life. I happen to be serious about Bunburying. What on earth you are serious about I haven't got the remotest idea. About everything, I should fancy. You have such an absolutely trivial nature.

JACK Well, the only small satisfaction I have in the whole of

this wretched business is that your friend Bunbury is
quite exploded. You won't be able to run down to
the country quite so often as you used to do, dear
Algy. And a very good thing too.

ALGERNON   Your brother is a little off colour, isn't he, dear Jack?
You won't be able to disappear to London quite so
frequently as your wicked custom was. And not a
bad thing either.

JACK   As for your conduct towards Miss Cardew, I must
say that your taking in a sweet, simple, innocent girl
like that is quite inexcusable. To say nothing of the
fact that she is my ward.

ALGERNON   I can see no possible defence at all for your
deceiving a brilliant, clever, thoroughly experienced
young lady like Miss Fairfax. To say nothing of the
fact that she is my cousin.

JACK   I wanted to be engaged to Gwendolen, that is all. I
love her.

ALGERNON   Well, I simply wanted to be engaged to Cecily. I
adore her.

JACK   There is certainly no chance of your marrying Miss
Cardew.

ALGERNON   I don't mind there is much likelihood, Jack, of you
and Miss Fairfax being united.

JACK   Well, that is no business of yours.

ALGERNON   If it was my business, I wouldn't talk about it.
(*Begins to eat muffins.*) It is very vulgar to talk
about one's business. Only people like stockbrokers
do that, and then merely at dinner parties.

JACK   How you can sit there, calmly eating muffins when
we are in this horrible trouble, I can't make out.
You seem to me to be perfectly heartless.

ALGERNON   Well, I can't eat muffins in an agitated manner. The
butter would probably get on my cuffs. One should
always eat muffins quite calmly. It is the only way
to eat them.

JACK   I say it's perfectly heartless your eating muffins at all, under the circumstances.

ALGERNON   When I am in trouble, eating is the only thing that consoles me. Indeed, when I am in really great trouble, as anyone who knows me intimately will tell you, I refuse everything except food and drink. At the present moment I am eating muffins because I am unhappy. Besides, I am particularly fond of muffins. (*Rising*)

JACK   (*rising*) Well, that is no reason why you should eat them all in that greedy way. (*Takes muffins from* ALGERNON.)

ALGERNON   (*offering tea-cake*) I wish you would have tea-cake instead. I don't like tea-cake.

JACK   Good heavens! I suppose a man may eat his own muffins in his own garden.

ALGERNON   But you have just said it was perfectly heartless to eat muffins.

JACK   I said it was perfectly heartless of you, under the circumstances. That is a very different thing.

ALGERNON   That may be. But the muffins are the same. (*He seizes the muffin-dish from* JACK.)

JACK   Algy, I wish to goodness you would go.

ALGERNON   You can't possibly ask me to go without having some dinner. It's absurd. I never go without my dinner. No one ever does, except vegetarians and people like that. Besides I have just made arrangements with Dr Chasuble to be christened at a quarter to six under the name of Ernest.

JACK   My dear fellow, the sooner you give up that nonsense the better. I made arrangements this morning with Dr Chasuble to be christened myself at 5.30, and I naturally will take the name of Ernest. Gwendolen would wish it. We can't both be christened Ernest. It's absurd. Besides, I have a perfect right to be christened if I like. There is no evidence at all that I ever have been christened by anybody. I should think it extremely probable I never was, and so does

Dr Chasuble. It is entirely different in your case. You have been christened already.

ALGERNON Yes, but I have not been christened for years.

JACK Yes, but you have been christened. That is the important thing.

ALGERNON Quite so. So I know my constitution can stand it. If you are not quite sure about your ever having been christened, I must say I think it rather dangerous your venturing on it now. It might make you very unwell. You can hardly have forgotten that someone very closely connected with you was very nearly carried off this week in Paris by a severe chill.

JACK Yes, but you said yourself that a severe chill was not hereditary.

ALGERNON It usen't to be, I know — but I daresay it is now. Science is always making wonderful improvements in things.

JACK (*picking up the muffin-dish*) Oh, that is nonsense; you are always talking nonsense.

ALGERNON Jack, you are at the muffins again! I wish you wouldn't. There are only two left. (*Takes them.*) I told you I was particularly fond of muffins.

JACK But I hate tea-cake.

ALGERNON Why on earth then do you allow tea-cake to be served up for your guests? What ideas you have of hospitality!

JACK Algernon! I have already told you to go. I don't want you here. Why don't you go!

ALGERNON I haven't quite finished my tea yet! and there is still one muffin left! (JACK *groans, and sinks into a chair.* ALGERNON *still continues eating.*)

ACT-DROP

ACT THREE

The morning-room at the Manor House. GWENDOLEN
and CECILY *are at the window, looking out into the
garden.*

GWENDOLEN The fact that they did not follow us at once into the
house, as anyone else would have done, seems to
me to show that they have some sense of shame left.

CECILY They have been eating muffins. That looks like
repentance.

GWENDOLEN (*after a pause*) They don't seem to notice us at all.
Couldn't you cough.

CECILY But I haven't got a cough.

GWENDOLEN They're looking at us. What effrontery!

CECILY They're approaching. That's very forward of them.

GWENDOLEN Let us preserve a dignified silence.

CECILY Certainly. It's the only thing to do now. (*Enter* JACK
followed by ALGERNON. *They whistle some dreadful
popular air from a British Opera.*)

GWENDOLEN This dignified silence seems to produce an
unpleasant effect.

CECILY A most distasteful one.

GWENDOLEN But we will not be the first to speak.

CECILY Certainly not.

GWENDOLEN Mr Worthing, I have something very particular to ask
you. Much depends on your reply.

CECILY Gwendolen, your common sense is invaluable. Mr
Moncrieff, kindly answer me the following question.
Why did you pretend to be my guardian's brother?

ALGERNON   In order that I might have an opportunity of meeting you.

CECILY   (*to* GWENDOLEN) That certainly seems a satisfactory explanation, does it not?

GWENDOLEN   Yes, dear, if you can believe him.

CECILY   I don't. But that does not affect the wonderful beauty of his answer.

GWENDOLEN   True. In matters of grave importance, style, not sincerity is the vital thing. Mr Worthing, what explanation can you offer to me for pretending to have a brother? Was it in order that you might have an opportunity of coming up to town to see me as often as possible?

JACK   Can you doubt it, Miss Fairfax?

GWENDOLEN   I have the gravest doubts upon the subject. But I intend to crush them. This is not the moment for German scepticism. (*Moving to* CECILY.) Their explanations appear to be quite satisfactory, especially Mr Worthing's. That seems to me to have the stamp of truth upon it.

CECILY   I am more than content with what Mr Moncrieff said. His voice alone inspires one with absolute credulity.

GWENDOLEN   Then you think we should forgive them?

CECILY   Yes. I mean no.

GWENDOLEN   True! I had forgotten. There are principles at stake that one cannot surrender. Which of us should tell them? The task is not a pleasant one.

CECILY   Could we not both speak at the same time

GWENDOLEN   An excellent idea! I nearly always speak at the same time as other people. Will you take the time from me?

CECILY   Certainly. (GWENDOLEN *beats time with uplifted finger.*)

GWENDOLEN and **CECILY**   (*speaking together*) Your Christian names are still an insuperable barrier. That is all!

JACK and **ALGERNON**   (*speaking together*) Our Christian names! Is that all? But we are going to be christened this afternoon.

GWENDOLEN (*to* JACK) For my sake you are prepared to do this terrible thing?

JACK I am.

CECILY (*to* ALGERNON) To please me you are ready to face this fearful ordeal?

ALGERNON I am!

GWENDOLEN How absurd to talk of the equality of the sexes! Where questions of self-sacrifice are concerned, men are infinitely beyond us.

JACK We are. (*Clasps hands with* ALGERNON.)

CECILY They have moments of physical courage of which we women know absolutely nothing.

GWENDOLEN (*to* JACK) Darling!

ALGERNON (*to* CECILY) Darling. (*They fall into each other's arms. Enter* MERRIMAN. *When he enters he coughs loudly, seeing the situation.*)

MERRIMAN Ahem! Ahem! Lady Bracknell!

JACK Good heavens! (*Enter* LADY BRACKNELL. *The couples separate in alarm. Exit* MERRIMAN.)

LADY B. Gwendolen! What does this mean?

GWENDOLEN Merely that I am engaged to be married to Mr Worthing, mamma.

LADY B. Come here. Sit down. Sit down immediately. Hesitation of any kind is a sign of mental decay in the young, of physical weakness in the old. (*Turns to* JACK.) Apprised, sir, of my daughter's sudden flight by her trusty maid, whose confidence I purchased by means of a small coin, I followed her at once by a luggage train. Her unhappy father is, I am glad to say, under the impression that she is attending a more than usually lengthy lecture by the University Extension Scheme on the Influence of a permanent income on Thought. I do not propose to undeceive him. Indeed I have never undeceived him on any question. I would consider it wrong. But of course, you will clearly understand that all communication between yourself and my daughter must cease immediately from this moment. On this point, as indeed on all points, I am firm.

JACK I am engaged to be married to Gwendolen, Lady Bracknell!

LADY B. You are nothing of the kind, sir. And now, as regards Algernon! ... Algernon!

ALGERNON Yes, Aunt Augusta.

LADY B. May I ask if it is in this house that your invalid friend Mr Bunbury resides?

ALGERNON (*stammering*) Oh! No! Bunbury doesn't live here. Bunbury is somewhere else at present. In fact, Bunbury is dead.

LADY B. Dead! When did Mr Bunbury die? His death must have been extremely sudden.

ALGERNON (*airily*) Oh! I killed Bunbury this afternoon. I mean poor Bunbury died this afternoon.

LADY B. What did he die of?

ALGERNON Bunbury? Oh, he was quite exploded.

LADY B. Exploded! Was he the victim of a revolutionary outrage. I was not aware that Mr Bunbury was interested in social legislation. If so, he is well punished for his morbidity.

ALGERNON My dear Aunt Augusta, I mean he was found out! The doctors found out that Bunbury could not live, that is what I mean — so Bunbury died.

LADY B. He seems to have had great confidence in the opinion of his physicians. I am glad, however, that he made up his mind at the last to some definite course of action, and acted under proper medical advice. And now that we have finally got rid of this Mr Bunbury, may I ask, Mr Worthing, who is that young person whose hand my nephew Algernon is now holding in what seems to me a peculiarly unnecessary manner?

JACK That lady is Miss Cecily Cardew, my ward. (LADY BRACKNELL *bows coldly to* CECILY).

ALGERNON I am engaged to be married to Cecily, Aunt Augusta.

LADY B. I beg your pardon?

CECILY Mr Moncrieff and I are engaged to be married, Lady Bracknell.

LADY B. (*with a shiver, crossing to the sofa and sitting down*) I do not know whether there is anything peculiarly exciting in the air of this particular part of Hertfordshire, but the number of engagements that go on seems to me considerably above the proper average that statistics have laid down for our guidance. I think some preliminary enquiry on my part would not be out of place. Mr Worthing, is Miss Cardew at all connected with any of the larger railway stations in London? I merely desire information. Until yesterday I had no idea that there were any families or persons whose origin was a Terminus. (JACK *looks perfectly furious, but restrains himself.*)

JACK (*in a clear, cold voice*) Miss Cardew is the granddaughter of the late Mr Thomas Cardew of 149, Belgrave Square, S.W.; Gervase Park, Dorking, Surrey; and the Sporran, Fifeshire, N.B.

LADY B. That sounds not unsatisfactory. Three addresses always inspire confidence, even in tradesmen. But what proof have I of their authenticity?

JACK I have carefully preserved the Court Guides of the period. They are open to your inspection, Lady Bracknell.

LADY B. (*grimly*) I have known strange errors in that publication.

JACK Miss Cardew's family solicitors are Messrs Markby, Markby, and Markby.

LADY B. Markby, Markby, and Markby? A firm of the very highest position in their profession. Indeed I am told that one of the Mr Markbys is occasionally to be seen at dinner parties. So far I am satisfied.

JACK   (*very irritably*) How extremely kind of you, Lady
       Bracknell! I have also in my possession, you will be
       pleased to hear, certificates of Miss Cardew's birth,
       baptism, whooping cough, registration, vaccination,
       confirmation, and the measles; both the German
       and the English variety.

LADY B.   Ah! A life crowded with incident, I see; though
       perhaps somewhat too exciting for a young girl. I am
       not myself in favour of premature experiences. (*Rises,
       looks at her watch.*) Gwendolen! the time approaches
       for our departure.We have not a moment to lose. As
       a matter of form, Mr Worthing, I had better ask you if
       Miss Cardew has any little fortune?

JACK   Oh! about a hundred and thirty thousand pounds in
       the Funds. That is all. Good-bye, Lady Bracknell. So
       pleased to have seen you.

LADY B.   (*sitting down again*) A moment, Mr Worthing. A
       hundred and thirty thousand pounds! And in the
       Funds! Miss Cardew seems to me a most attractive
       young lady, now that I look at her. Few girls of the
       present day have any really solid qualities, any of
       the qualities that last, and improve with time. We
       live, I regret to say, in an age of surfaces.
       (*To* CECILY.) Come over here, dear. (CECILY *goes
       across.*) Pretty child! your dress is sadly simple, and
       your hair seems almost as Nature might have left it.
       But we can soon alter that. A thoroughly experienced
       French maid produces a really marvellous result in a
       very brief space of time. I remember recommending
       one to young Lady Lancing, and after three months
       her own husband did not know her.

JACK   (*aside*) And after six months nobody knew her.

LADY B.   (*glares at* JACK *for a few moments. Then bends,
       with a practised smile, to* CECILY.) Kindly turn
       round, sweet child. (CECILY *turns completely
       round.*) No, the side view is what I want. (CECILY
       presents her profile.) Yes, quite as I expected.
       There are distinct social possibilities in your

profile. The two weak points in our age are its want of principle and its want of profile. The chin a little higher, dear. Style largely depends on the way the chin is worn. They are worn very high, just at present. Algernon!

ALGERNON Yes, Aunt Augusta!

LADY B. There are distinct social possibilities in Miss Cardew's profile.

ALGERNON Cecily is the sweetest, dearest, prettiest girl in the whole world. And I don't care twopence about social possibilities.

LADY B. Never speak disrespectfully of Society, Algernon. Only people who can't get into it do that. (*To* CECILY.) Dear child, of course you know that Algernon has nothing but his debts to depend upon. But I do not approve of mercenary marriages. When I married Lord Bracknell I had no fortune of any kind. But I never dreamed for a moment of allowing that to stand in my way. Well, I suppose I must give my consent.

ALGERNON Thank you, Aunt Augusta.

LADY B. Cecily, you may kiss me!

CECILY (*kisses her*) Thank you, Lady Bracknell.

LADY B. You may also address me as Aunt Augusta for the future.

CECILY Thank you, Aunt Augusta.

LADY B. The marriage, I think, had better take place quite soon.

ALGERNON Thank you, Aunt Augusta.

CECILY Thank you, Aunt Augusta.

LADY B. To speak frankly, I am not in favour of long engagements. They give people the opportunity of finding out each other's character before marriage, which I think is never advisable.

JACK I beg your pardon for interrupting you, Lady Bracknell, but this engagement is quite out of the question. I am Miss Cardew's guardian, and she cannot marry without my consent until she comes of age. That consent I absolutely decline to give.

LADY B.   Upon what grounds may I ask? Algernon is an extremely, I may almost say an ostentatiously, eligible young man. He has nothing, but he looks everything. What more can one desire?

JACK   It pains me very much to have to speak frankly to you, Lady Bracknell, about your nephew, but the fact is that I do not approve at all of his moral character. I suspect him of being untruthful. (ALGERNON *and* CECILY *look at him in indignant amazement.*)

LADY B.   Untruthful! My nephew Algernon? Impossible! He is an Oxonian.

JACK   I fear there can be no possible doubt about the matter. This afternoon, during my temporary absence in London on an important question of romance, he obtained admission to my house by means of the false pretence of being my brother. Under an assumed name he drank, I've just been informed by my butler, an entire pint bottle of my Perrier-Jouet, Brut, '89; a wine I was specially reserving for myself. Continuing his disgraceful deception, he succeeded in the course of the afternoon in alienating the affections of my only ward. He subsequently stayed to tea, and devoured every single muffin. And what makes his conduct all the more heartless is, that he was perfectly well aware from the first that I have no brother, that I never had a brother, and that I don't intend to have a brother, not even of any kind. I distinctly told him so myself yesterday afternoon.

LADY B.   Ahem! Mr Worthing, after careful consideration I have decided entirely to overlook my nephew's conduct to you.

JACK   That is very generous of you, Lady Bracknell. My own decision, however, is unalterable. I decline to give my consent.

- **LADY B.** (*to* CECILY) Come here, sweet child. (CECILY *goes over.*) How old are you, dear?

- **CECILY** Well, I am really only eighteen, but I always admit to twenty when I go to evening parties.

- **LADY B.** You are perfectly right in making some slight alteration. Indeed no woman should ever be quite accurate about her age. It looks so calculating ... (*In a meditative manner.*) Eighteen, but admitting to twenty at evening parties. Well, it will not be very long before you are of age and free from the restraints of tutelage. So I don't think your guardian's consent is, after all, a matter of any importance.

- **JACK** Pray excuse me, Lady Bracknell, for interrupting you again, but it is only fair to tell you that according to the terms of her grandfather's will Miss Cardew does not come legally of age until she is thirty-five.

- **LADY B.** That does not seem to me to be a grave objection. Thirty-five is a very attractive age. London society is full of women of the very highest birth who have, of their own free choice, remained thirty-five for years. Lady Dumbleton is an instance in point. To my own knowledge she has been thirty-five ever since she arrived at the age of forty, which was many years ago now. I see no reason why our dear Cecily should not be even more attractive at the age you mention than she is at present. There will be a large accumulation of property.

- **CECILY** Algy, could you wait for me till I was thirty–five?

- **ALGERNON** Of course I could, Cecily. You know I could.

- **CECILY** Yes, I felt it instinctively, but I couldn't wait all that time. I hate waiting even five minutes for anybody. It always makes me rather cross. I am not punctual myself, I know, but I do like punctuality in others, and waiting, even to be married, is quite out of the question.

- **ALGERNON** Then what is to be done, Cecily?

- **CECILY** I don't know, Mr Moncrieff.

LADY B.   My dear Mr Worthing, as Miss Cardew states positively that she cannot wait till she is thirty-five – a remark which I am bound to say seems to me to show a somewhat impatient nature – I would beg of you to reconsider your decision.

JACK   But my dear Lady Bracknell, the matter is entirely in your own hands. The moment you consent to my marriage with Gwendolen, I will most gladly allow your nephew to form an alliance with my ward.

LADY B.   (*rising and drawing herself up*) You must be quite aware that what you propose is out of the question.

JACK   Then a passionate celibacy is all that any of us can look forward to.

LADY B.   That is not the destiny I propose for Gwendolen. Algernon, of course, can choose for himself. (*Pulls out her watch.*) Come, dear; (GWENDOLEN *rises*) we have already missed five, if not six, trains. To miss any more might expose us to comment on the platform. (*Enter* DR CHASUBLE.)

CHASUBLE   Everything is quite ready for the christenings.

LADY B.   The christenings, sir! Is not that somewhat premature?

CHASUBLE   (*looking rather puzzled, and pointing to* JACK *and* ALGERNON) Both these gentlemen have expressed a desire for immediate baptism.

LADY B.   At their age? The idea is grotesque and irreligious! Algernon, I forbid you to be baptised. I will not hear of such excesses. Lord Bracknell would be highly displeased if he learned that that was the way in which you wasted your time and money.

CHASUBLE   Am I to understand then that there are to be no christenings at all this afternoon?

JACK   I don't think that, as things are now, it would be of much practical value to either of us, Dr Chasuble.

CHASUBLE   I am grieved to hear such sentiments from you,

Mr Worthing. They savour of the heretical views of the Anabaptists, views that I have completely refuted in four of my unpublished sermons. However, as your present mood seems to be one peculiarly secular, I will return to the church at once. Indeed, I have just been informed by the pew-opener that for the last hour and a half Miss Prism has been waiting for me in the vestry.

LADY B. (*starting*) Miss Prism! Did I hear you mention a Miss Prism?

CHASUBLE Yes, Lady Bracknell. I am on my way to join her.

LADY B. Pray allow me to detain you for a moment. This matter may prove to be one of vital importance to Lord Bracknell and myself. Is this Miss Prism a female of repellent aspect, remotely connected with education?

CHASUBLE (*somewhat indignantly*) She is the most cultivated of ladies, and the very picture of respectability.

LADY B. It is obviously the same person. May I ask what position she holds in your household?

CHASUBLE (*severely*) I am a celibate, madam.

JACK (*interposing*) Miss Prism, Lady Bracknell, has been for the last three years Miss Cardew's esteemed governess and valued companion.

LADY B. In spite of what I hear of her, I must see her at once. Let her be sent for.

CHASUBLE (*looking off*) She approaches; she is nigh. (*Enter* MISS PRISM *hurriedly.*)

MISS PRISM I was told you expected me in the vestry, dear Canon. I have been waiting for you there for an hour and three quarters. (*Catches sight of* LADY BRACKNELL *who has fixed her with a stony glare.* MISS PRISM *grows pale and quails. She looks anxiously round as if desirous to escape.*)

LADY B. (*in a severe, judicial voice*) Prism! (MISS PRISM *bows her head in shame.*) Come here, Prism! (MISS PRISM *approaches in a humble manner.*) Prism! Where is that baby? (*General consternation.* CHASUBLE *starts back in horror.* ALGERNON *and* JACK *pretend to be anxious to shield* CECILY *and* GWENDOLEN *from hearing the details of a terrible public scandal.*) Twenty-eight years ago, Prism, you left Lord Bracknell's house, Number 104, Upper Grosvenor Street, in charge of a perambulator that contained a baby, of the male sex. You never returned. A few weeks later, through the elaborate investigations of the Metropolitan police, the perambulator was discovered at midnight, standing by itself in a remote corner of Bayswater. It contained the manuscript of a three-volume novel of more than usually revolting sentimentality. (MISS PRISM *starts in involuntary indignation.*) But the baby was not there! (*Everyone looks at* MISS PRISM.) Prism! Where is that baby? (*A pause.*)

MISS PRISM Lady Bracknell, I admit with shame that I do not know. I only wish I did. The plain facts of the case are these. On the morning of the day you mention, a day that is for ever branded on my memory, I prepared as usual to take the baby out in its perambulator. I had also with me a somewhat old, but capacious handbag, in which I had intended to place the manuscripts of a work of fiction that I had written during my few unoccupied hours. In a moment of mental abstraction, for which I never can forgive myself, I deposited the manuscript in the bassinette, and placed the baby in the handbag.

JACK (*who has been listening attentively*) But where did you deposit the handbag?

MISS PRISM Do not ask me, Mr Worthing.

JACK Miss Prism, this is a matter of no small importance to me. I insist on knowing where you deposited the handbag that contained that infant.

MISS PRISM I left it in the cloakroom of one of the larger railway stations in London.

JACK What railway station?

MISS PRISM (*quite crushed*) Victoria. The Brighton line. (*Sinks into a chair.*)

JACK I must retire to my room for a moment. Gwendolen, wait here for me,

GWENDOLEN If you are not too long, I will wait here for you all my life. (*Exit* JACK *in great excitement.*)

CHASUBLE What do you think this means, Lady Bracknell?

LADY B. I dare not even suspect, Dr Chasuble. I need hardly tell you that in families of high position strange coincidences are not supposed to occur. They are hardly considered the thing.

Noises heard overhead as if someone was throwing trunks about. Everyone looks up.

CECILY Uncle Jack seems strangely agitated.

CHASUBLE Your guardian has a very emotional nature.

LADY B. This noise is extremely unpleasant. It sounds as if he was having an argument. I dislike arguments of any kind. They are always vulgar, and often convincing.

CHASUBLE (*looking up*) It has stopped now. (*The noise is redoubled.*)

LADY B. I wish he would arrive at some conclusion.

GWENDOLEN This suspense is terrible. I hope it will last. *Enter* JACK *with a handbag of black leather in his hand.*

JACK (*rushing over to* MISS PRISM) Is this the handbag, Miss Prism? Examine it carefully before you speak. The happiness of more than one life depends on your answer.

MISS PRISM (*calmly*) It seems to be mine. Yes, here is the injury it received through the upsetting of a Gower Street omnibus in younger and happier days. Here is the stain on the lining caused by the explosion of a temperance beverage, an incident that occurred at Leamington. And here, on the lock, are my initials. I had forgotten that in an extravagant mood I had had them placed there. The bag is

undoubtedly mine. I am delighted to have it so
unexpectedly restored to me. It has been a great
inconvenience being without it all these years.

JACK (*in a pathetic voice*) Miss Prism, more is restored to
you than this handbag. I was the baby you placed
in it.

MISS PRISM (*amazed*) You?

JACK (*embracing her*) Yes ... mother!

MISS PRISM (*recoiling in indignant astonishment*) Mr Worthing!
I am unmarried!

JACK Unmarried! I do not deny that is a serious blow. But
after all, who has the right to cast a stone against
one who has suffered? Cannot repentance wipe out
an act of folly? Why should there be one law for
men, and another for women? Mother, I forgive you.
(*Tries to embrace her again.*)

MISS PRISM (*still more indignant*) Mr Worthing, there is some
error. (*Pointing to* LADY BRACKNELL.) There is the lady
who can tell you who you really are.

JACK (*after a pause*) Lady Bracknell, I hate to seem
inquisitive, but would you kindly inform me who I
am?

LADY B. I am afraid that the news I have to give you will not
altogether please you. You are the son of my poor
sister, Mrs Moncrieff, and consequently Algernon's
elder brother.

JACK Algy's elder brother! Then I have a brother after all. I
knew I had a brother! I always said I had a brother!
Cecily — how could you have ever doubted that I
had a brother? (*Seizes hold of* ALGERNON.) Dr Chasuble,
my unfortunate brother. Miss Prism, my unfortunate
brother. Gwendolen, my unfortunate brother. Algy,
you young scoundrel, you will have to treat me with
more respect in the future. You have never behaved
to me like a brother in all my life.

ALGERNON Well, not till today, old boy, I admit. I did my best,
however, though I was out of practice. (*Shakes
hands.*)

GWENDOLEN (*to* JACK) My own! But what own are you?

What is your Christian name, now that you have
become someone else?

JACK Good heavens! ... I had quite forgotten that point.
Your decision on the subject of my name is
irrevocable, I suppose?

GWENDOLEN I never change, except in my affections.

CECILY What a noble nature you have, Gwendolen!

JACK Then the question had better be cleared up at once.
Aunt Augusta, a moment. At the time when Miss
Prism left me in the handbag, had I been christened
already?

LADY B. Every luxury that money could buy, including
christening, had been lavished on you by your fond
and doting parents.

JACK Then I was christened! That is settled. Now, what
name was I given? Let me know the worst.

LADY B. Being the eldest son you were naturally christened
after your father.

JACK (*irritably*) Yes, but what was my father's Christian
name?

LADY B. (*meditatively*) I cannot at the present moment recall
what the General's Christian name was. But I have
no doubt he had one. He was eccentric, I admit.
But only in later years. And that was the result of
the Indian climate, and marriage, and indigestion,
and other things of that kind.

JACK Algy! Can't you recollect what our father's Christian
name was?

ALGERNON My dear boy, we were never even on speaking
terms. He died before I was a year old.

JACK His name would appear in the Army Lists of the
period, I suppose, Aunt Augusta?

LADY B. The General was essentially a man of peace, except
in his domestic life. But I have no doubt his name
would appear in any military directory.

JACK The Army Lists of the last forty years are here. These delightful records should have been my constant study. (*Rushes to bookcase and tears the books out.*) M. Generals ... Mallam, Maxbohm, Magley, what ghastly names they have – Markby, Migsby, Mobbs, Moncrieff! Lieutenant 1840, Captain Lieutenant-Colonel, Colonel, General 1869, Christian names, Ernest John. (*Puts book very quietly down and speaks quite calmly.*) I always told you, Gwendolen, my name was Ernest, didn't I? Well, it is Ernest after all. I mean it naturally is Ernest.

LADY B.   Yes, I remember now that the General was called Ernest. I knew I had some particular reason for disliking the name.

GWENDOLEN   Ernest! My own Ernest! I felt from the first that you could have no other name!

JACK   Gwendolen, it is a terrible thing for a man to find out suddenly that all his life he has been speaking nothing but the truth. Can you forgive me?

GWENDOLEN   I can. For I feel that you are sure to change.

JACK   My own one!

CHASUBLE   (*to* MISS PRISM) Lætitia! (*Embraces her.*)

MISS PRISM   (*enthusiastically*) Frederick! At last!

ALGERNON   Cecily! (*Embraces her.*) At last!

JACK   Gwendolen! (*Embraces her.*) At last!

LADY B.   My nephew, you seem to be displaying signs of triviality.

JACK   On the contrary, Aunt Augusta, I've now realized for the first time in my life the vital Importance of Being Earnest.

CURTAIN

QUESTIONS AND EXPLORATIONS

1 Keeping Track

The questions in this section are designed to help your reading and understanding of the play in the areas of plot, character, interaction and structure. They may be used as you read the play or afterwards, for discussion or for writing. Some are developed and expanded in the *Explorations* section.

Act One

1 What should the audience see at the start of Act One?

2 How should Lane arrange the afternoon tea?

3 What is Algernon's attitude to Lane? How would he show it? Also, how would Lane show his attitude to Algernon?

4 What do we learn about Jack's background? Who is Ernest?

5 What is Algernon's opinion of romance and marriage?

6 How does Jack react when Algernon teases him about Cecily?

7 Who is Bunbury? Why is he important to Algernon?

8 Summarise the nature of the relationship between Jack and Algernon.

9 What type of a woman is Lady Bracknell? How would she behave?

10 What is Gwendolen's attitude to Jack? How would she show it?

11 What is the problem Gwendolen poses for Jack?

12 How would Lady Bracknell react upon re-entering.

13 Why does Lady Bracknell interrogate Jack?

14 What is Jack's true background found to be?

15 How does Lady Bracknell react to this news?

16 What does Jack decide to do about his brother 'Ernest'?

17 What do we learn about Cecily?

18 Why does Gwendolen return?

19 What is Algernon planning to do at the end of Act One?

Act Two

1 What should the audience see at the start of Act Two?

2 What type of governess is Miss Prism? How would this be shown?

3 What sort of person is Cecily? How would this be shown?

4 What impression of Jack are we given by Miss Prism and Cecily?

5 What are Miss Prism's and Canon Chasuble's reactions to each other?

6 Why does Algernon pretend to be Jack's brother Ernest?

7 How do Algernon and Cecily react to each other?

8 How would the audience react to Jack's news that Ernest is dead?

9 Why does Jack wish to be christened?

10 What is Cecily's reaction on seeing Jack?

11 What is Jack's reaction to seeing 'Ernest' at the Manor House?

12 Why is the conversation between Jack and 'Ernest' amusing?

13 How does Jack treat Algernon once the other characters have left?

14 How does Algernon feel about Cecily?

15 What are Algernon's reactions to Cecily's news of her engagement to 'Ernest', to her diaries and to her letters from 'Ernest'?

16 What is Cecily's reaction to Gwendolen?

17 And what is Gwendolen's reaction to Cecily?

18 What is the cause of Cecily's and Gwendolen's confusion over their engagement to 'Ernest'?

19 How does this confusion change their attitudes to each other?

20 How would the taking of afternoon tea be conducted?

21 How do Cecily and Gwendolen react to Algernon and Jack's return?

22 How do Jack and Algernon react to the situation?

23 How and why do their attitudes to each other change by the end of Act Two?

Act Three

1 What would the audience see at the beginning of Act Three?

2 What is the atmosphere between the two couples?

3 How easily are Cecily and Gwendolen convinced by Jack and Algernon's explanation? Why?

4 How does the atmosphere change with Lady Bracknell's arrival?

5 How does Lady Bracknell react to the news of the engagements?

6 Why does Lady Bracknell decide not to leave after all?

7 Why does Jack refuse his consent to Algernon marrying Cecily?

8 What effect does Canon Chasuble's entry have upon the scene?

9 How do Lady Bracknell and Miss Prism react to each other?

10 How do the others react to Lady Bracknell's interrogation of Miss Prism? What does it reveal?

11 How does Jack react to Miss Prism's story?

12 How does Miss Prism react to Jack's embrace?

13 How does Jack react to the discovery that he is Algernon's brother? How would this reaction be shown?

14 How would Algernon react to the news?

15 How does Jack react upon discovering his true name?

16 How would an audience react to the climax of the play?

2 Explorations

The questions in this section are more detailed and rely on your having read the whole play. Some of the questions develop ideas from the *Keeping Track* section. Because they tend to be more detailed, they offer the opportunity to develop the ideas into written, oral or practical coursework assignments. Some will require a close knowledge of the play; others will require a more imaginative response.

A Characters

1 Select one of the major characters. Referring to the text as appropriate, show your selected character's attitudes both to themselves and to others.

2 How vividly created are the characters of the play? Give evidence from the play in your answer.

3 How 'real' are the characters of the play? What are Wilde's priorities in characterisation?

4 With reference to the text, show the nature of one selected character from the play. How successfully is s/he created?

5 Create a monologue for a selected character from the play in which s/he reflects upon the events of the play. How will s/he react and express him/herself?

6 What are the functions of the various characters in the play? Show how their interaction drives the plot.

B Themes

1 'It is very romantic to be in love'. What are the various characters' attitudes to romance?

2 'Oh, pleasure, pleasure. What else should bring anyone anywhere?' How do the various characters in the play please themselves?

3 'If ever I get married, I'll certainly try to forget the fact'. What attitudes to marriage are expressed in the play? How far do those attitudes change?

4 'A gross deception has been practised on both of us'. Give examples of how mistaken identity adds to the humour of the play.

5 'The truth is rarely pure and never simple'. Show how the misunderstandings in the plot are resolved.

6 'Oh, that is nonsense; you are always talking nonsense'. Giving examples, show how epigram and paradox contribute to the humour of the play.

7 *The Importance of Being Earnest* is a 'trivial comedy for serious people'. What aspects of late Victorian society does Wilde seek to mock and trivialise?

C In Performance

1 Select one of the acts of the play. Using the stage directions at the start of the act, draw up a set design brief. What furniture and props would be required? How would you dress the set to create the atmosphere Wilde intended?

2 Select one of the major characters. What aspects of that character would you need, as an actor, to highlight for the benefit of an audience? How would you use voice, gesture and movement to achieve this?

3 Select an extract from the play. How would you direct that extract in order to make it successful for an audience? Refer to speech, movement, expression and interaction as appropriate.

4 What costumes are required for a period performance of the play? Draw up a costume design brief, with costume ideas for a selected character from the play.

5 Show how you would realise the humour of the play for the benefit of an audience.

6 Design and create a poster for a production of the play at your local theatre. Consider how to attract and interest a potential audience: explain your choice and presentation of design.

D Criticism

1 What were Wilde's intentions in writing *The Importance of Being Earnest*?

2 'The characters are unreal and fail to evoke our interest'. How far do you agree with this statement?

3 *The Importance of Being Earnest* is 'as devoid of purpose as a paper balloon'. How fair is this description of the play?

4 Giving detailed reference to the text, analyse the humour of the play.

5 What in the play do the characters take seriously? What do they treat as triviality?

6 'Everything matters in art, except the subject'. What mattered to Wilde in creating and writing the play?

7 'Everything matters in art, except the subject'. What, in your opinion, is the subject of the play?

Bibliography

Plays

The major plays of Oscar Wilde, including *Lady Windermere's Fan, A Woman of No Importance* and *An Ideal Husband*, are all available in:

Wilde: The Complete Plays

ed. H. Montgomery Hyde **Methuen 1988**

In addition, the Four Act Version of *The Importance of Being Earnest* is also published by Methuen.

Bibliography

Oscar Wilde	Richard Ellman	**Hamish Hamilton/ Penguin 1987**
Oscar Wilde	H. Montgomery Hyde	**Methuen 1976**
Oscar Wilde	Martin Fido	**Hamlyn 1973**

Criticism

A wide range of critical work focuses upon Wilde. Start with:

Oscar Wilde: *The Critical Heritage*	ed. K. Beckson	**RKP 1970**
File on Wilde	ed. Margery Morgan	**Methuen 1990**
Oscar Wilde	Katherine Worth	**Macmillan 1983**

General

The Revels History of Drama in English Vol VII	ed. T.W. Craik	**Methuen 1978**